To Marog
from
Mother Duffield

Dec 25 1954

Mrs HANNAH MORE

M.W. DODD.

HANNAH MORE

OR

Life in Hall and Cottage

BY

Mrs. HELEN C. KNIGHT,

BARLEY WOOD THE RESIDENCE OF THE LATE HANNAH MORE.

NEW YORK:

PUBLISHED BY M. W. DODD.

1851.

A

NEW MEMOIR

OF

HANNAH MORE;

OR

Life in Hall and Cottage.

BY

MRS. HELEN C. KNIGHT.

NEW YORK:
PUBLISHED BY M. W. DODD,
BRICK CHURCH CHAPEL, CITY HALL SQUARE,
(OPPOSITE THE CITY HALL.)
1853.

STEREOTYPED BY THOMAS B. SMITH,
216 WILLIAM STREET, N. Y.

CONTENTS.

CHAPTER I.

CHAPTER VIII.

CHAPTER IX.

CHAPTER X.

CHAPTER XI.

CHAPTER XII.

CHAPTER XIII.

CHAPTER XIV.

CHAPTER XV.

CHAPTER XVI.

PREFACE.

————◆•◆————

IT has been written, "that the world's wealth
is its original men; by these and their works, it
is a world and not a waste: the memory and record of what *men* it bore—this is the sum of its
strength, its 'sacred property' forever, whereby
it upholds itself and steers forward, better or
worse, through the yet undiscovered deep of time.

" Science itself, is it not, under one of its most
interesting aspects, Biography? Is it not the record of the *work*, which an original man, still
named by us or not named, was blessed by the
heavens to do?"

May it not be also said, that the wealth of the
Church is her godly men, her holy women, her
ransomed little ones? Are not the record and
memory of their self-denial and suffering, their
patient waiting, and cheerful courage, their faith

1*

and love, her richest legacies and dearest treasures? By these is the world an Eden and not a waste; by these is the Church the true vine and not a withered branch; a living epistle and not a dead letter; the memory and record of what *Christian men* and *women* it bore—this is the sum of her strength, her " sacred property" forever.

Christianity itself, is it not under one of its most interesting aspects, *biography?* Is it not the record of the *work*, which a God-man was blessed by the heavens to do? Have not its doctrines been unfolded by the lives and labors of its eminent disciples?

In this view, what meaning is there in the christian life, whenever bearing " precious fruit," within the cottage or the hall, in the little child patiently bearing its weary load for Christ's sake, or in those holy and devout ones, whose faith subdued kingdoms, wrought righteousness, and having obtained a good report, have gone to receive their great recompense of reward.

Herein is the beauty and excellency of the life of this eminent servant of God, Hannah More.

Among the household memories, if not among

the nursery rhymes of many in middle life, she is
less known to a great multitude of the young, who
are just entering upon the duties, the responsibili-
ties, and conflicts of the christian life, and for
them is this sketch prepared. If there is a tendency in the Church, as some fear, to consult
worldly advantages more than Christ's requirements, to be content with a weak faith and feeble
hopes, instead of the warm, large, generous love
which inspired the apostles of old, and eminent
saints of later time, to rest satisfied with only a
name to live, instead of bringing forth fruits meet
for repentance, let us turn back and study the
characters of those whose lips and lives most eloquently expressed the holy gospel they professed.
Let us inquire what doctrines they believed, what
principles they adopted, what duties they dis-
charged, what labors they undertook, what amusements they forsook; in a word, let us seek to find
out their apprehension of Bible truth, and how
also the Bible shaped their views, moulded their
characters, and fitted them for usefulness. Hannah More presents one of the most complete mod-
els of christian character; her life is a beautiful
development of that healthy, vigorous, life-giving,

and heart-warming piety, which springs from the distinguishing doctrines of the Bible, cordially believed and faithfully acted upon. Let every American woman study her biography. It is a legacy left for our benefit; a portrait for our contemplation; an example to imitate; a token for encouragement and hope; an earnest of that fulness in Christ Jesus, "if we do show the same diligence to the full assurance of hope unto the end, that we be not slothful, but followers of them who through faith and patience inherit the promises."

CHAPTER I.

Early Days.

LET us visit the retired hamlet of Fishponds; it is in the parish of Stapleton, four miles from Bristol, and possesses all the quiet and homely comfort of rural life in England. Among the humble homes of the hamlet, stands that of the Dominie, Mr. Jacob More, a man of piety and learning, who, though bred to larger expectations and an ampler inheritance, is the faithful and contented master of the parish school, the happy husband of his excellent Mary, the proud father of five little girls, and the thankful proprietor of valuable stock in domestic peace and enjoyment. He is a devoted member of the English Church, and a loyal subject of good King George. The over-cast fortunes of his early days, and the mansion and estates of Wenhaston wrested from him in a suit at law, are well-nigh forgotten amid the manifold cares and busy interests of family rearing. Besides leading a flock of village urchins to nibble in the green pastures of knowledge, his five little girls follow the same friendly crook, and in their training, he beholds the buds and blossoms, as he hopes to realize the fruit, of his professional skill and parental fidelity.

With more enlarged views of female education than were common an hundred years ago, when external accomplishments were principally aimed at, good Mr. More, though not without a certain horror for a learned lady, determined to strengthen the minds of his daughters by a thorough course of study, and to enlarge their range of thought by well-selected reading : his object was to fit them for usefulness, in whatever sphere the Providence of God might direct their steps.

The home influences which surrounded this band of sisters were the purest and the best : not harassed by poverty, or stricken by luxury, but surrounded by the steady, yet gentle, pressure of *ever doing*, they were early taught the wonderful power of the " diligent hand ;" away from the fevered excitements, and fashionable trickery of city life, they only knew life through the simple and frugal habits of their parents, enriched and beautified by the clear sense and devout spirit of their mother, and by the classic tastes and well-stored mind of their father. There also, was the English culture, which every English child sucks as from its mother's milk, veneration for the time-worn and time-honored institutions of his fathers ; the warm glow of loyal affection clustering and centering around a royal household, the obedient heart doing homage to the lofty prerogatives of priestly power, joy and pride over his English soil dotted all over with monuments of historic truth and great men's doings. Those elements which shape the national character, and in a greater or less degree mark and strengthen the individual influence, are perhaps modified since an hundred years ago, although they must ever exercise a strong and decided influence over every true-born English child.

As the sisters passed from infancy to childhood, from childhood to maidenhood, the daily discipline of reading and grammar, of Latin and mathematics, was diversified and relieved by household labors and rural exercises.

To the studies, which fell within Mr. More's own province, he wished to add that of the French language, and for this purpose, when Mary, the eldest, was twelve, she went three times a week to Bristol to receive lessons from the most approved instructors, in order to fit her to become the teacher of her younger sisters : through hot and cold, through wet and dry, with a resolution which ever afterward was one of the most prominent traits in her character, Mary More trod unweariedly her solitary four miles' walk, studying with unflinching earnestness until she became a thorough master of the French, and spoke it with the fluency and elegance of a native.

While the eldest daughter was thus toiling up the hill of knowledge, Elizabeth, next her in age, was busy by her mother's side, plying the needle, turning the wheel, or adding to family comfort through the thousand unseen channels of simple duties and little kindnesses.

Then came Sarah, brimful of wit and humor, whose quaint sayings and lively answers were the delight of her companions, and often provoked a smile from the Dominie in his gravest and most thoughtful moods.

Having lost a valuable portion of his library on his mournful pilgrimage from the paternal estate, Mr. More was constrained to teach history in the more animated style of conversation and story; and his own interest in Grecian sages and Roman heroes was revived and quickened by the bright eyes and earnest glance of his fourth little one, ever first on her father's knee, listening with a glowing face to the wonderful recitals which fell from his lips. While still regarded as "the little one," and long before she was thought worthy of the paternal teaching, the delighted parents were surprised to find her reading with intelligence and fluency, having slipped through the long apprenticeship of syllables and spelling, they hardly knew. when, or how.

The little one had no mind to wait the slow notice of her elders. She learned while they spake one to another, as it were, from the droppings which fell unawares upon her eager and panting spirit; a scrap of paper and an old pen are among her baby-house treasures; in rude characters she attempts to put down the thoughts which spring up abundantly within her little bosom. Before her father's door was the high road which leadeth to the great city, Bristol, with its manifold and far-off wonders; the child, perhaps, often sits and ponders whence it comes and whither it goes, eagerly watching the heavy carts, or the pillion equestrians as they occasionally pass and repass,—each suggesting a new fancy, or pleasing wonder; as she ponders, she writes dainty thoughts. Behold, the little child of four years is a rhymer—perhaps a poet!—

> "This is the road to a great city
> Which is more populous than witty,"

is all that survives of this, her earliest essay, through the long lapse of years. Beside the poem, her fourth year has other marvels for expectant and loving kindred. The

2

village curate awards her sixpence for catechism lessons
well learned and perfectly recited :—her first *earned* sixpence, her *own* sixpence—how rich is the little one !—
rich in the curate's approval and fatherly hopes ! rich in
promise ! Such were the first laurels of the Dominie's
fourth, Hannah More, born in the year 1745.

Her father, delighted with the dawning abilities of the
child, soon began to teach her his favorite Latin ;
amazed at her rapid progress, he abandoned the work,
lest Hannah should grow up a pedant ; this, however,
he willingly resumed, not long after, at the entreaty of the
child, seconded by the persuasions of the mother.   The
little Hannah was henceforth permitted to read, study and
write, as her fancy led ; her scribblings were of divers
sorts and kinds ; poems, essays, and stories issued from
her pen, and were stored away to be read or recited to
her sisters, whose encouragement and interest at that
early age, fostered and improved her taste.

Patty was the youngest of the flock, loving and joyous, never jealous of the opening powers of her sister,
for whom her admiration was only equalled by her warm
sisterly love.

As the family grew up, its increasing wants outran its
straitened means, when the elder sisters proposed to

follow the profession of their father, and try the experiment of a new boarding-school in the neighboring city.

Warm friends, who knew their worth, seconded the plan, and offered their patronage and influence: among their patrons was Mrs. Gwatkin, a lady of worth and high position, who then little dreamed that through the friendly aid she rendered to this band of teachers, her own name should be handed to generations yet to come. The family circle was now broken up. Mary, Elizabeth, and Sarah left the paternal roof to try their fortunes in the great world: the school was opened; scholars flocked to this fold, and the first year confirmed their hopes and encouraged farther efforts. With what solicitude and pride must the father have watched their progress in the same ordeal of daily struggles, in which he had already become a veteran; and when at last at the age of twelve he suffered the little Hannah to escape from his nest, and become a pupil in the now prosperous school, he gave the strongest proof which a father could give, of confidence in, and respect for the abilities of his daughters for their new and responsible situation.

What a world of interest opened upon the gifted girl in the wider sphere of study and observation, in the diversity of character, in the new friendships and associations, in the competitions and struggles of school life in the city. The green banks, the shady groves and soft quiet of Stapleton, gave place to the stirring and endless passing to and fro of people, of scenes, of labors : what a quickening of thought! what incitements and stimulas ! She was not among strangers who, caring not, crowded her mind, or cramped her heart; she was not a stray lamb in a strange fold, but affection still folded her in its bosom, defending her from harmful flatteries, and rejoicing in her opening and maturing powers. Her progress was brilliant and rapid, reflecting honor upon the school, and attracting the attention of some of the most cultivated minds in the city. Sir James Stonehouse, a friend and patron of her sisters, whose writings for the spiritual benefit of the sick have been extensively circulated in the Society for Promoting Christian Knowledge, became deeply interested in her welfare; he took every opportunity of cultivating the young girl's friendship, and while yet a pupil, predicted her distinguished career.

Beside Sir James, Dr. Tucker, afterwards Dean of Gloucestershire, Mr. Peach, a man of extensive reading and fine taste, and Ferguson, the astronomer, then lecturing at Bristol, sought her society with delight, and were reckoned among her warmest friends. So great, at that early period, were the charms of her conversation, that Dr. Woodward, her physician, a man of some eminence in his time, is said one day altogether to have forgotten she was his patient, while she regaled his ear with strains it seemed a privilege to hear, until half way down stairs, he suddenly recollected himself, exclaiming, "Bless me! I forgot to ask the girl how she was!" while he hastened back to her chamber to make the necessary inquiries.

Hannah's literary tastes showed themselves in her pastimes, as well as in her graver pursuits, for we learn that a favorite play at one time among herself and companions, was the gathering of little parties, where the talk should be wholly sustained in the language of Shakspeare, and "it was surprising," she said in after days, " how well the conversation was kept up." It must be remembered that children's literature had then no existence ; the Parent's Assistant, Sanford and Merton, Harry and Lucy, books which a few years afterward delighted and quickened the minds of the young, had not then appeared, nor had Mrs. Barbauld, or Mrs. Trimmer, yet employed their pens in the juvenile department, at once so unambitious and yet so useful and important. Children read then—if they read at all—books which their elders read and loved,

2*

and Shakspeare, it seems, must have been among the choice reading of young Hannah More: this unwonted appreciation of, and intimate acquaintance with his writings, was the means of imparting to one of her earliest journeys a zest and enjoyment which few, at her early age, could have been supposed to feel.

In company with some friends, she visited Stratford-upon-the-Avon, the birth-place of the immortal and world-renowned poet, and brought away a branch of the mulberry-tree growing in his garden, said to have been planted by his own hand; this she had wrought into sugar-tongs and presented to Mrs. Gwatkin, with the verse—

> "I kissed the sacred shrine where Shakspeare lay,
> And bore this relic of my bard away:
> Where shall I place it, Phœbus ?—where 'tis due,
> Apollo answered: and I send it—*you*."

At seventeen a small work issued from her pen, entitled "The Search after Happiness," a pastoral drama, which, with an ever-grateful sense of Mrs. Gwatkin's kindness to her family, she dedicated to that lady. Acting plays was at that time one branch of boarding-school instruction, and this was written to take the place of those, of which class there were not a few, not always inculcating the purest sentiments, or the most exalted character : however well it may have answered its purpose, and however great its literary merits were then regarded by admiring and expectant friends, it can hardly now be considered prophetic of anything but the high moral aim which it was the tendency of her maturer efforts to inculcate and to enforce.

Unexpected success had crowned the efforts of the sisters : the faithful and judicious management of the home department, together with the superior course of instruction given in the school, gave it a deservedly high position in the community, and attracted pupils from the most distant parts of the kingdom. The sisters determined now to enlarge their domain, and for this purpose they planned and built a large and commodious house in Park-street, where, notwithstanding their ampler accommodations, twice the number of applicants appeared than could possibly be admitted.

Nor were they unmindful of the comfort, and increasing infirmities of their now only remaining parent. Mr. More, bereft of his family, was by their filial love removed to a pleasant house in the city, and provided with two female servants to attend him, where he passed a green old age, in the enjoyment of his garden, his library, his friends, and, above all, the daily visits and delightful companionship of his five excellent daughters.

After having completed her studies as pupil, Hannah retained her connection in the school as teacher. Beloved and respected in no common degree, the younger sisters were often invited by their pupils to visit their homes during the vacation recesses. They were, at this time, on an intimate footing with the Misses Turner, two older members of the school, and were often invited to accompany them to Belmont, the residence of their cousin, Edward Turner, Esq., six miles from Bristol. The fine taste and cultivated mind of Hannah made a strong impression on the host, who delighted to consult her in his projected improvements, and followed her suggestions in many of the embellishments made at this time on his estate ;—nor did she fail to find themes for her muse in the shady nooks and green winding ways of beautiful Belmont. On the summit of a hill reached by a steep and rugged path through the woods, in whose deep seclusion we may suppose she sometimes loved to linger, there remained, long after her death, a board over-written with a little poem, to inspire the weary pilgrim with hope and resolution through his tedious and rugged way, suggested by the nature of the scenery around her. In erecting a monument to a departed friend, Mr. Turner was indebted to his guest for the inscription it bears, and which afterward appeared in her works under the title "Inscription on a Cenotaph," and it is no matter of surprise, that one so fitted to sympathize with him in his tastes and pursuits, should have engaged his affection, and, for a time, at least, have wooed him from his love of single life. Though twice her age, for Hannah was now nearly twenty-two, he sought her hand; the suit was favorably regarded, and the bridal preliminaries were completed, when the current of true love, not always smoothly flowing, drifted them apart, and sundered the tie; nor does it appear that Hannah ever afterwards freighted her bark on the same dangerous element.

The gentleman never ceased to regard her with respect and interest, and his first toast every day, whether alone, or in society, ever was "Hannah More." In after years, their long-suspended intercourse was renewed, and continued with the utmost cordiality until his death, when he bequeathed to her a thousand pounds. There are no tearful regrets to bestow over this severed tie, for Mrs. Turner might have deprived the world of the brilliant career and valuable services of Miss Hannah More. She

afterwards received an offer of marriage from Dr. Lang-
horne, vicar of Blagdon, author of several works, a man
of lively wit and cultivated intellect, with whom she became acquainted while in quest of health and strength on
the coast of Somersetshire. Behold her on the beach,
sometimes on a pillion behind her servant, sometimes ac-
coutered for a walk in company with the Doctor, sometimes surrounded by a group of admiring friends, drawn
thither by the charms of her brilliant and animated conversation. Though a rejected suitor, the Doctor maintained a poetical and literary correspondence with the
lady until his death, which took place in the prime of
manhood, although not before his usefulness had become
blighted by irregularities and misfortune.

Thus far have we caught passing glimpses of Hannah
More in the dear seclusion of her birth-place, the busy
retreat of her sisters' school, and the agreeable circle of
Bristol society, where her simple manners, her good sense,
and the unaffected friendliness of her heart, gave an
added lustre to those brilliant powers and that ready wit,
which, afterwards, made her a welcome and honored
guest in the most elegant and refined circles of the metropolis. How much is there in her early life of which
the few and scanty records that remain, fail to inform

us! How many an earnest mother would rend the veil
which conceals her childhood to learn the secret springs
of that Christian nurture, which enabled her to pass
unseduced and unscathed through the trying ordeal
of folly, of fashion, and of fame which awaited her.
The glitter and pomp of fashionable life never seems to
have dimmed the clearness of her moral vision, or prevented her from making a rational estimate of its maxims,
habits, and pursuits; there ever accompanied her an integrity of moral consciousness, a hidden strength, which
stronger than breast-plate or shield, defended her from the
corrupting influence of flattery, and enabled her to maintain that singleness and purity of character, and to foster
those religious convictions which formed the beauty and
excellence of her riper years.

CHAPTER II.

Introduction to London Society.

BRILLIANT minds centre around this period of English literature. The splendid diction of Burke had kindled a fresh glow around "The Sublime and Beautiful;" the Deserted Village was surrounded by admiring groups: Johnson fed and fattened the world of letters from the storehouse of his strong and affluent mind; Sir Joshua Reynolds was in the zenith of his popularity; and Garrick, the enchanter of the English, ruled the stage.

London society was rife with genius, wit, and learning: the famous Blue Stocking Club was then in its glory, and its accomplished patrons figured in the most elegant and refined circles of that day. This gathering, which has unwittingly given a name of implied reproach to women of literary tastes and pursuits, was composed of persons distinguished for wit and talent, who met at each other's houses, without ceremony or supper, to enjoy the charm of each other's society, without the interloping aid of cards or dancing, as we learn from a little poem entitled the Bas Bleu, written by Hannah More a few years after—

> " Long was society o'errun
>   By Whist, that desecrating Hun,
>   Long did Quadrille despotic sit,
>   That Vandal of colloquial wit,
>   And conversation's setting light
>   Lay deep obscured in Gothic night;
>   At length the mental shades decline;
>   Colloquial wit begins to shine;
>   Genius prevails, and conversation
>   Emerges into reformation."

An object befitting the cultivated minds of that day, when speech, we may suppose " to have been the golden harvest that followed the flowing of thought :" an object too which it might not be amiss to revive, if, in the feverish reading, and rapid flight of news, people can pause and think; for, without thought, that healthy digestment of things worthy to be known, conversation must soon lose its freshness and originality, and degenerate into mere news-telling and literary gossip.

Among the admired women of that circle ranks **Mrs.** Elizabeth Montagu, who acquired much celebrity as the

author of an "Essay on the Genius of Shakspeare," published in 1769, of which Cowper says, "The learning, the
good sense, the sound judgment, and the wit displayed in
it, fully justify, not only my compliment, but all compli-
ments, either that have already been paid to her talents,
or shall be paid hereafter:" but while the Essay which
made her conspicuous to her contemporaries has passed
away, she became better known in this country by a
volume of her delightful letters, which charmed the reading world fifty years ago. Beautiful in youth, and left in
possession of an ample fortune at the death of her husband, she retained, until the latest period of life, a grace
of person and manner, which made her splendid mansion
at Berkeley Square a centre of the most polished society in
the metropolis. By her side, behold Elizabeth Carter,
accounted one of the most learned ladies of her time, the
long-loved and intimate companion of Mrs. Montagu. At
twenty-nine, Dr. Johnson, whom no one would venture to
call an indiscriminate admirer of the sex, in a fit of unusual gallantry, composed a Greek epigram to her praise;
and she was almost the only lady, through long years of
intercourse, whom he treated with uniform attention and
civility. For the encouragement of the young, who are
more ready to question their abilities than to exercise

them, and for the benefit of teachers who are impatient of progress which they are not faithful enough to secure, let it be added, that Mr. Carter, in early days Elizabeth's instructor, became so wearied and disheartened by the dulness and apparent stupidity of his daughter, that he abandoned the task of teaching her, while she, with a resolution which nothing could quench, continued her studies until she became a thorough master of the learned languages. Dr. Johnson, in speaking of a celebrated Greek scholar, said he understood Greek better than anybody else, except Elizabeth Carter: the Bible, her choicest book, she was accustomed to read in Hebrew: the fishermen of Deal, her place of residence except during her long absences at London, respectfully regarded her as the *almanac maker*, that being the highest conception they could form of the abilities and power of their distinguished townswoman. Her biography may be found in some of our older libraries, together with "Mrs. Chapone's Letters to Young Ladies," a famous book in its day, upon which the dust of years has already gathered. No lady could afford to be without its wise counsel and judicious guidance: anxious and careful mothers gave it to their young daughters; and so popular was the aid which it rendered to parents, that it became the maternal ancestor of a long

line of "Letters to the Young," it being through no want
of advisers or lack of advice, if the young of our generation are not vastly wiser and better than their elders were.

Here is Mrs. Chapone, one of the Blue Stocking coterie,
with another, no less distinguished in her day, Hon. Frances Boscawen, widow of Admiral Boscawen, the warm and
appreciating friend of literary worth and rising genius.
With her comes Mrs. Vesey, to whom, in pleasing remembrance of the delightful gatherings so often enjoyed at her
house, Miss More dedicated her Bas Bleu poem,

> "Vesey! of sense the judge and friend,
> Awhile my idle strains attend."

Brilliant as these circles were, enriched by the learning
of Johnson, the wit of Garrick, the taste of Reynolds, the
elegance of Mrs. Montagu, and the moral worth of Elizabeth Carter, they were yet to receive a delightful accession
in the gifted woman, who, in company with her sister
Sarah, left Bristol on a visit to London, in the winter of
1773, and began, as she says, for the first time, to " know
something of the hurry, bustle, dissipation, and nonsen-
sical flutter of town life."

Her reputation had already preceded her, and Hannah
More is soon a guest at the table of Sir Joshua Reynolds,

whose handsome establishment in Leicester-fields was the resort of the gay and learned. Hosts of friends surrounded his hospitable board, drawn thither quite as much by the genial warmth of his spirit as by the world-wide reputation of his genius, and the monuments of his industry and art. His sister Frances presided over his house, with whom Hannah was speedily on an intimate footing. Miss Reynolds, if we may credit a contemporary critic, seems not to have been a very skilful housewife, or to have served her brother's table with an especial reference to order or arrangement, there often being a deficiency of knives, forks, plates, and glasses; yet their friends long loved the memory of those social hours, which, after the sun had set that gave them warmth, no one ever attempted to revive or imitate.

We next follow her to Hampton Court, the princely domain of Cardinal Woolsey, located in the midst of an extensive park of majestic trees, sixteen miles from London. Here were the chambers of royalty, with their superb pictures and ancient tapestry; here the beauties of King William's court, looking beautiful still through the stiff and antique drapery of elder times: here, too, the records of royal industry, tapestry wrought by Queen Mary's hands, when, surrounded by her maidens, "her

3*

needle plied its busy task." Although this seat of historical interest and royal magnificence could not fail to interest, her youthful enthusiasm was quickened to a warmer glow by a visit to the "immortal shades" of Twickenham, the abode, both in life and death, of Pope, one of her favorite authors, and at the distance of only a pleasant walk from Hampton Court.

The curious domain of the poet, at that time in possession of Sir William Stanhope, had suffered few outward changes; the rooms had been stripped of every memento of its former occupant: his bust, statue, pictures, and library, many of them gifts of distinguished men, and tributes to his genius, had been scattered far and wide among his friends, but the house remained, with its curiously wrought arcades, columns, and porticos. The garden, shrubbery, and grotto were also there, where Addison, Swift, Parnel, and Bolingbroke read, wrought, wrote and raked, far from the busy and distracting scenes of London life; nor could she leave without plucking a sprig of laurel from the garden, and stealing two stones from the grotto, in memory of the great departed: neither did she leave Twickenham, without visiting the hallowed tomb of her "beloved bard," who quietly rests in the village church, beneath a stone bearing the inscription, "One who would not be buried in Westminster Abbey," he, as Hannah wittily suggested, probably preferring to be the first ghost in Twickenham than an inferior one at Westminster.

On her return to Hampton, she visited the country house of David Garrick, beautifully situated on the Thames, and then undergoing some repairs. She wandered over his grounds, and stole into his temple, a quiet garden retreat, containing, among other things, a chair, curiously wrought from the tree which grew in Shakspeare's garden.

"I sat in it," wrote she to Mrs. Gwatkins, "but caught no inspiration. What drew my attention most was a splendid statue of that great and original man, in an attitude strikingly pensive; his limbs strongly muscular, his countenance expressive of some vast conception, and his whole form seeming the bigger from some immense idea, with which you suppose his imagination pregnant. The statue cost £500."

With a kindred spirit did she dwell upon the storied honors and fair renown of those, whose haunt was upon the lips of men, and whose dwelling was in their heart.

The drama was then a favorite department of literature with Hannah More: her first article was dramatic, and she had already sketched some of the most grand and thrill-

ing scenes in Hebrew history, which afterward appeared
in the form of the "Sacred Dramas." No wonder, then,
that Garrick was at once an object of curiosity and deep
interest; and she longed to witness those remarkable gifts,
fitted

> "To pierce, to cleave, to tear the heart,
>   Whatever names delight the ear,
>   Othello, Richard, Hamlet bear."

She first beheld him in the character of King Lear,
and her graphic description of his powers, in a letter to
a mutual friend, evincing a just appreciation, and a correct
criticism of the drama, inspired him at once with the
strongest desire to see and know her.

David Garrick was at that time master of the English
stage: though somewhat past the prime of life, having
nearly reached his sixtieth year, his frame still retained
the flexibility and vigor of earlier days. With genius
and refinement, "the finest man in the world for sprightly
conversation," as Johnson says, whose pupil he had been,
and whose friendship he ever continued to enjoy, Garrick's
house, adorned by Eva Maria, his beautiful and accomplished wife, was a centre of attraction to the literary
circles of that period.

Of the versatility of his talent, some idea may be formed from the famous couplet of Goldsmith,

"Our Garrick's a salad, for in him we can see
Oil, vinegar, sugar, and saltness agree."

An introduction soon followed: the interview imparted mutual pleasure, and the foundations of a warm and cordial intimacy were laid, which lasted until his death. Garrick immediately introduced his new friend into the elegant circle over which Mrs. Montagu presided: she soon became a frequent guest at Berkeley Square, and the intimate companion of many of the choice spirits of that day.

But Hannah, with whetted appetite, longed to behold the wonder of the age, "Irene Johnson!" "Dictionary Johnson!" "Idler, Rambler Johnson!" nor did her wishes remain long ungratified. Calling one day at Sir Joshua's, she learned he was within: her friends tried to moderate her eagerness, by telling her of the moody fits of the Doctor, in which he would be quite as likely to turn his back, or think of Tom Thumb, as on another occasion, to give her a befitting welcome. How agreeably disappointed was she, on entering the room where he was, to find herself greeted with the utmost cordiality, by a verse

of her own poetry, while he arose to receive her, with
Sir Joshua's maccaw jauntily perched on his arm: the
maccaw, indeed, was a great favorite with the Doctor,
whose fame has extended to our own times, by its appreciating estimate of young Northcote's work. While a
pupil at Sir Joshua's studio, he took a portrait of one of
the servants, which being brought into the room where
the bird happened to be, it mistook it for the original,
against whom it harbored a grudge, and instantly flew
to the canvass with the greatest fury; nor could it ever
contemplate the picture without a similar exhibition of
feeling. Hannah was most favorably impressed with the
great conversationist; and not long afterwards, she and
her sister Sarah paid him a visit at his own lodgings, in
company with Miss Reynolds. On entering his little parlor, they found it occupied by a pale, shrunken old lady,
dressed in scarlet, her head surmounted by a black lace
hood, with stiff projecting wings: she received them with
a mild and engaging manner, and bade them be seated.
Hannah promptly obeyed, by jumping into a great arm-
chair, which she naturally concluded could be nobody's
accustomed seat but the Doctor's, and playfully invoking
the inspiration of his genius.

Their hostess was Miss Anna Williams, the blind poetess, who for forty years was sheltered beneath the Doctor's roof. The daughter of an early friend, on coming up to London, before his wife's death, for the purpose of having an operation performed upon her eyes, she was invited to become a guest at their house during Mrs. Johnson's illness. She was the companion of her sick chamber, and after her death, failing to receive the expected benefit from medical aid, Dr. Johnson, in pity to her desolate situation, offered her a home. Her destitute situation enlisted the sympathy of his friends, and she became a pensioner upon their bounty. Garrick gave her a benefit, which settled upon her £200. Mrs. Montagu allowed her ten pounds a year, and Miss Carter aided in getting up a subscription for her poems, which amounted to nearly £1500 more. Thus, though her book has long since ceased to make any claim upon the reading world, Miss Williams is destined to immortality through the generosity of her benefactor, and the liberality of his friends.

Hark! the heavy tread of the host is at the door: he enters: behold his burly and unwieldy body, his face disfigured by scrofula, and head surrounded by a large, bushy, grayish wig, well singed, or, perhaps, quite crisp in front—a very fright to the respectable company of wigs with which it daily associates: its master's eyes are both weak and near-sighted, which, in his absorbing interest for a favorite author, often cause him to bring the light within a dangerous vicinity to his person, quite regardless of consequences. When he dined with distinguished guests at Leicester-fields, Sir Joshua's butler used to take the liberty of drawing the Doctor aside, and replacing the old wig with one more suitable to the occasion.

He is dressed in plain brown clothes, black worsted stockings, and silver knee-buckles. His rolling gait, with the odd and convulsive twists of his unwieldy body, added to a harsh and imperious voice, altogether formed a personelle sufficiently disagreeable to repulse the least fastidious; but with all those defects and infirmities of the outward man, Dr. Johnson was the intellectual Hercules of his age.

> "Subtle when strong, invincible when right,
> Armed at all points, and glorying in his might;
> Gladiator-like, he traverses the field,
> And strength and skill compel the foe to yield."

Of the Doctor, in a softer light, the poet adds—

> "And I have seen him with a milder air,
> Encircled with the witty and the fair,

> Even in old age, with placid mien rejoice
> At beauty's smile, and beauty's flattering voice."

At the time of Hannah's introduction to him, he was past sixty-five, bearing the accumulated infirmities of age and disease, though keenly alive as ever to the pleasures of tea and conversation. No person, probably, enjoyed with more relish that cup which cheers, but not inebriates, or possessed a more appreciative sense of the qualities of Bohea.

Come early or late, the tea-table was sure to be spread. By the friendly inspiration of the fragrant leaf, his morning was endured, his evenings were solaced, and he could talk the twenty-four hours together without weariness or rest, did not a considerate regard to the bed-time of his friends release them from his side.

"I lie down," he once said, "that my acquaintance might sleep, for I lie down to endure oppressive misery, and soon rise again to pass the night in anxiety and pain." Of poor Johnson it might be said, that bodily existence was a torture.

As he enters now the little parlor in Fleet-street, the comers are received with friendly warmth; he laughs heartily at Hannah, and declares that in the big arm-chair he never sits.

4

Perhaps they discuss his "Journey to the Hebrides," just published, a work which shows the fertility of his mind, in investing the dryest subject with interest, and turning the most barren spot to a profitable account, four thousand copies of the work having been sold on the first week of its publication.

On Hannah's return to Bristol, in 1774, her feelings became warmly enlisted for her favorite candidate in the Parliament election, which was then going on, Hon. Edmund Burke, who made the friendship, and was a frequent guest of the Misses More. When success at the polls became more than probable, the sisters presented him with their congratulatory addresses, through a splendid cockade, composed of the sublime and beautiful colors analyzed in his famous essay, entwined with myrtle and ivy, laurel and bay, decorated with silver tassels, and filled with appropriate mottoes, two of which are the following:

"He is himself the great sublime he draws."
"In action faithful, and in honor clear."

The box was handed him while surrounded by a large company, which being opened, the cockade came to light, amid the applauses of his friends, and the universal inquiry whence the tribute came. Burke himself declared

it could only be from his Park-street friends. It was
elevated to a conspicuous situation in the committee-room,
until his success became undisputed, when it graced his
cap on the day of his triumph.

CHAPTER III.

𝔄 𝔓𝔢𝔢𝔭 𝔞𝔱 𝔱𝔥𝔢 𝔅𝔩𝔲𝔢𝔰.

THE bright world of intellectual life and social elegance, into which Hannah More was suddenly and unexpectedly ushered, while it brought her into companionship with people whom it was a pleasure and a privilege to know, also brought her into contact with amusements and habits, which were not only foreign to her tastes, but opposed to her moral sense; though indulged in and enjoyed by her new friends and admirers, she is not dazzled by their example, or seduced into an approval contrary to her convictions.

In her free home letters, so full of good sense and graphic description, she opens a loophole into her heart and habits, through which we see the great and gifted in the easy and every-day dress of social and familiar intercourse.

The following was written during her second visit to London, in 1775:

"Our visit was at Sir Joshua's, where we were received

with all the friendship imaginable. I am going to-day to a great dinner: nothing can be conceived so absurd, extravagant, and fantastical, as the present mode of dressing the head. Simplicity and modesty are things so much exploded, that their very names are no longer remembered. I have just escaped from one of the fashionable disfigurers, and though I charged him to dress me with the greatest simplicity, and to have only a very distant eye upon the fashion, just enough to avoid the pride of singularity; yet in spite of all these sage cautions, I absolutely blush at myself, and turn to the glass with as much caution as a vain beauty just risen from the small-pox, which cannot be a more disfiguring disease than the present mode of dress. Of the one, the calamity may be greater in its consequences, but of the other, it is more corrupt in its cause.

"We have been reading a treatise on the morality of Shakspeare. It is a happy and easy way of filling a book that the present race of authors have arrived at—that of criticising the works of some eminent poet; with monstrous extracts and short remarks. It is a species of cookery that I begin to grow tired of: they cut up their authors in chops, and by adding a little crumbled bread of their own, and tossing it up a little, they present it as a fresh dish: you are to dine upon the poet; the critic supplies the garnish, yet has the credit, as well as the profit, of the whole entertainment."

LONDON, 1775.

I had yesterday the pleasure of dining in Hill-street, Berkeley Square, at a certain Mrs. Montagu's, a name not totally obscure. The party consisted of herself, Mrs. Carter, Dr. Johnson, Salander, and Matty, Mrs. Boscawen, Miss Reynolds, and Sir Joshua (the idol of every company), some other persons of high rank and less wit, and your humble servant—a party that would not have disgraced the table of Lelius or of Atticus. I felt myself a worm, the more a worm for the consequence which was given me, by mixing me with such a society; but, as I told Mrs. Boscawen, and with great truth, I had an opportunity of making an experiment of my heart, by which I learned that I was not envious; for I certainly did not repine at being the meanest person in company.

Mrs. Montagu received me with the most encouraging kindness: she is not only the finest genius, but the finest lady I ever saw. She lives in the highest style of magnificence; her apartments and table are in the most splendid taste; but what baubles are these, when speaking of a Montagu! her form (for she has no *body*) is delicate

even to fragility; her countenance the most animated in
the world; the sprightly vivacity of fifteen, with the judgment and experience of a Nestor. But I fear she is hastening to decay very fast. Her spirits are so active, that they
must soon wear out the little frail receptacle that holds
them. Mrs. Carter has in her person a great deal of what
the gentlemen mean when they say, such a one is a
" poetical lady :" however, independently of her great
talents and learning, I like her much : she has affability,
kindness, and goodness ; and I honor her heart even more
than her talents. But I do not like one of them better
than Mrs. Boscawen : she is at once polite, learned, judicious, and humble ; and Mrs. Palk tells me, her letters are
not thought inferior to Mrs. Montagu's. She regretted
(so did I), that so many suns could not possibly shine
at one time : but we are to have a smaller party, where,
from fewer luminaries, there may emanate a clearer, stead-
ier, and more beneficial light. Dr. Johnson asked me how
I liked the new tragedy of Braganze. I was afraid to
speak before company : however, as I thought it a less
evil to dissent from the opinion of a fellow-creature, than
to tell a falsity, I ventured to give my sentiments ; and
was satisfied with Johnson's answering, " you are right,
madam."

With sisterly pride, and in a tone of affectionate eulogy, Sarah, who joined Hannah in her winter sojourning at London, thus writes, in her bright and lively style, to the sisterhood at Bristol:

LONDON, 1775.

Tuesday evening we drank tea at Sir Joshua's, with Dr. Johnson. Hannah is certainly a great favorite. She was placed next him, and they had the entire conversation to themselves. They were both in remarkably high spirits: it was certainly her lucky night! I never heard her say so many good things. The old genius was extremely jocular, and the young one very pleasant. You would have imagined we had been at some comedy, had you heard our peals of laughter. They, indeed, tried which could "pepper the highest," and it is not clear to me that the lexicographer was really the highest seasoner. Yesterday, Mr. Garrick called upon us; a volume of Pope lay upon the table: we asked him to read, and he went through the latter part of the "Essay on Man." He was exceedingly good-humored, and expressed himself quite delighted with our eager desire for information; and when he had satisfied our interrogatory, "Now, madam, what next?" He read several lines we had been disputing about, with regard to emphasis, in many different ways, before he decided which was right. He sat with us from half-past twelve till three, reading and criticising. We have just had a call from Mr. Burke.

LONDON, 1775.

> "Bear me, some god, O quickly bear me hence,
> To wholesome solitude, the nurse of ——"

"Sense," I was going to add, in the words of Pope, till I recollected that *pence* had a more appropriate meaning, and was as good a rhyme. This apostrophe broke from me, writes Hannah, on coming from the opera, the first I ever *did*, the last, I trust, I ever *shall* go to. For what purpose has the Lord of the universe made his creature man with a comprehensive mind? why make him a little lower than the angels? why give him the faculty of thinking, the powers of wit and memory; and to crown all, an immortal and never-dying spirit? Why all this wondrous waste, this prodigality of bounty, if the mere animal senses of sight and hearing (by which he is not distinguished from the brutes that perish) would have answered the end as well; and yet I find that the same people are seen at the opera every night—an amusement written in a language the greater part of them do not understand, and performed by such a set of beings. But the man

"Who bade the reign commence
Of rescued nature and reviving sense,"

sat at my elbow, and reconciled me to my situation, not
by his approbation, but his presence. Going to the opera,
like getting drunk, is a sin that carries its own punishment
with it, and that a very severe one. Thank my dear Doctor Stonehouse for his kind and seasonable admonitions
on my last Sunday's engagement at Mrs. Montagu's.
Conscience had done its office before; nay, was busy at
the time; and if it did not dash the cup of pleasure to
the ground, infused at least a tincture of wormwood into
it. I *did* think of the alarming call, "What doest thou
here, Elijah?" and I thought of it to-night at the opera.

SUNDAY NIGHT, 9 o'clock.

Perhaps you will say, I ought to have thought of it
again to-day, when I tell you I have dined abroad; but it
is a day I reflect on without those uneasy sensations one
has, when one is conscious it has been spent in trifling
company. I have been at Mrs. Boscawen's. Mrs. Montagu, Mrs. Carter, Mrs. Chapone, and myself only were admitted. We spent the time, not as wits, but as reasonable
creatures; better characters, I trow. The conversation was
sprightly, but serious. I have not enjoyed an afternoon so

much since I have been in town. There was much sterling sense, and they are all ladies of high character for
piety, of which, however, I do not think their visiting on
Sunday any proof: for though their conversation is edifying, the example is bad.

The more I see of the "honored, famed, and great," the
more I see of the littleness, the unsatisfactoriness of all cre-
ated good, and that no earthly pleasure can fill up the
wants of the immortal principle within. One need go no
farther than the company I have just left, to be convinced
that "pain is for man," and that fortune, talents, and science, are no exemption from the universal lot. Mrs. Montagu, eminently distinguished for wit and virtue, "the
wisest where all are wise," is hastening to insensible decay
by a slow but sure hectic. Mrs. Chapone has experienced
the severest reverses of fortune; and Mrs. Boscawen's life
has been a continued series of afflictions, that may almost
bear a parallel with those of the righteous man of Uz.
Tell me, then, what is it to be wise? This, you will say,
is exhibiting the unfavorable side of the picture of humanity, but it is the right side, the side that shows the likeness.

CHAPTER IV.

Literary Blossomings.

WHILE Miss More was at home in the winter of 1775, she one day said to her sisters, "I have been so fed with praise, I think I will venture to try what my real value is, by writing a slight poem."

Her social position had been greatly changed since the Pastoral Drama issued from her pen, perhaps at the desk of the noisy school-room, beyond which her fame and influence were but just extending.

London and "live authors" were yet in the distance, lying in the warm sunlight of her youthful fancy, nor had her gayest hopes or wildest wishes or maturing powers foretold the honored destiny in store for her. Now, on the path of time, had she been out to meet it; the brilliant circles of London already delighted in her presence; wit, wealth, and learning, bade her welcome; her mind, quickened and enriched, asked for proof of the powers thus admired and valued by the great and gifted.

The Pastoral Drama even had become a favorite: a sixth edition had been called for, and it was this year published in Philadelphia, whence came two little poems in compliment to its author: the entire profits of the sale had netted £100.

Hannah resumed her pen, and within a fortnight, two poems were completed,—"Sir Eldred of the Bower," and "The Bleeding Rock." These, on her return to London, she presented to a well-known publisher, Cadell, who offered her forty guineas, promising at the same time, could she discover what Goldsmith received for his "Deserted Village," to increase the sum to that amount.

Of this flattering award of pounds and pence, the "Deserted Village" has now no right to feel envious, for it has a pepetual inheritance in our hearts, while "Sir Eldred," after a brief fondling from the great men of his day, has passed into obscurity and neglect.

Miss Sally More, who accompanied her sister to London, writes home the gratifying news—"From Miss Reynolds we learn, that Sir Eldred is the theme of conversation in all the polite circles, and that the beauteous Bertha has kindled a flame in the cold heart of Johnson, who declares, that her parent has but one fault, which is, suffering herself to graze upon the barren rocks of Bristol, while the

rich pastures of London are guarded by no fence which
could exclude her from them."

In another letter she adds : " If a wedding should take
place before our return, don't be surprised—between the
mother of Sir Eldred and the father of Irene—nay, Mrs.
Montagu says, if tender words are the precursors of connu-
bial engagements, we may expect great things ; for it is
nothing but 'child,' a 'little fool,' 'love,' and 'dearest.'
After much critical discourse, he turns round to me, and
with one of his most amiable looks, which must be seen to
form the least idea of, he says : ' I have heard you are engaged in the useful and honorable occupation of teaching
young ladies :' upon which, with all the ease, familiarity,
and confidence we should have done, had only our dear
Dr. Stonehouse been present, we entered upon the history
of our birth, parentage, and education, showing how we
were born with more desires than guineas, and how as years
increased our appetites, the cupboard, at length, began to
grow too small for them, and how with a bottle of water, a
bed and a blanket, we set out to seek our fortunes ; and
how we found a great house with nothing in it ; and how
it was like to remain so, till looking into our knowledge-
boxes, we happened to find a little learning a very good
thing, when land is gone—and so, at last, by giving a little

of this to those who had less, we got a good store of gold
in return—but how, alas, we wanted the wit to keep it.
'I love you both,' cried the Doctor. 'I love you all five!
I never was at Bristol; I will come on purpose to see you,
—what! five women live happily together! I will come
and see you. I have spent a happy evening; I am glad
I came; God forever keep you—you live to shame duch-
esses.' He took his leave with so much warmth and tenderness, we were quite affected by his manner."

The sisters visited Garrick at his beautiful rural residence at Hampton, where he entertained them by reading the whimsical correspondence in prose and verse, which
for many years he had carried on with the first geniuses
of that age.

"We see him now," says Patty, "in his mellower light,
when the world has been shaken off: he says, he longs to
enter into himself, and to study the more important duties
of life, which he is determined upon doing. The next time
we go, Hannah is to carry some of her writing; she is to
have a little table by herself, and to continue her studies,
while he does the same."

"I dined at the Adelphi yesterday," writes Hannah,
in one of her free home-letters, revealing so much of just
what it is pleasant to know. " It was a particular occa-

sion, an annual meeting, where nothing but men are usually asked. I, however, was of the party, and an agreeable day it was to me. I have seldom heard so much wit under the banner of so much decorum. Colman and Dr. Schomburg were of the party; the rest were chiefly old doctors of divinity. At six I begged leave to come home, as I expected a polite assembly a little after seven. They came at seven. The dramatis personæ were Mrs. Boscawen, Mrs. Garrick, and Miss Reynolds: my beaux were Dr. Johnson, Dean Tucker, and last, but not least in our love, David Garrick. You know that wherever Johnson is, the confinement to the tea-table is rather a durable situation, and it was an hour and a half before I got my enlargement. Garrick was the very soul of the company, and I never saw Johnson in such perfect good humor. Sally knows that we have often heard that one can never properly enjoy the company of these two unless they are together. There is great truth in this remark; for after the Dean and Mrs. Boscawen (who were the only strangers) were withdrawn, and the rest stood up to go, Johnson and Garrick began a close encounter, telling old stories, ' e'en from their boyish days,' at Litchfield. We all stood around them for above an hour, laughing in defiance of every rule of Chesterfield. Johnson outstaid them all, and sat with me half an hour."

At the repeated and urgent solicitations of the Garricks, Miss More soon after took up her abode at the Adelphia, their town house, of which she humorously says, "The master and mistress are sensible, well-behaved people, and keep good company; besides, they are fond of books, and can read, and have a shelf full, which they lend me. Add to this, it is not a common lodging-house: they are careful whom they take in; and will have no people of bad character, or who keep irregular hours."

"I have a great deal of time at my own disposal, to read my own books, and see my own friends; and whenever I please, may join in the most elegant and polished society in the world. Our breakfasts are little literary societies— there is generally company at meals, as they think it saves time, by avoiding the necessity of seeing people at other seasons. Mr. Garrick sets the highest value upon his time. I detest and avoid public places more than ever, and should make a miserably bad fine lady."

Some idea may be formed of her industry, that amid all the social attractions which surrounded her, she could find time to read four or five hours every day, and sometimes write ten.

5*

There is something heart-warming in the cordial and unfettered intercourse of Hannah and her London friends. The circle into which she had been thrown contained almost every element for social enjoyment: no circle, indeed, has been more famed for its colloquial powers, to which wit, learning, and refinement, good breeding, good nature, and good sense, made such unstinted contributions.

How pleasant is it to snatch these glimpses into the home-life of distinguished men, and to see them, as it were, in their every-day dress.

Miss More once said to Horace Walpole, " that the truest objects of warm attachment are the small parts of great characters," which, we cannot help thinking, comprehends a delightful truth. Who does not love Cowper taming his hares, or enjoy Johnson sipping his tea, or Pope at work in his garden?—when the abilities which inspired our admiration, and seemed to lift their possessor beyond the common reach of our sympathies, taketh pleasure in those " slender joys, which, often repeated, fall like sunshine on the soul."

"Let me tell you a ridiculous circumstance which happened the other day," writes Hannah, in one of her delightful home-letters. " After dinner Garrick took up the Monthly Review (civil gentlemen, by-the-bye, these monthly reviewers), and read 'Sir Eldred' with all his grace and pathos. I think I was never so ashamed in my life; but he read it so superlatively that I cried like a child. Only think, what a scandalous thing to cry at the reading of one's own poetry! I could have beaten myself; for it looked as if I thought it very moving, which, I can truly say, is far from being the case. But the beauty of the jest lies in this: Mrs. Garrick twinkled as well as I, and made as many apologies for crying at her husband's reading, as I did for crying at my own verses. *She* got out of the scrape, by pretending that she was touched by the story, and *I* by saying the same thing of the reading. It furnished us a great laugh at the catastrophe, when it really would have been decent to have been a little more sorrowful."

In spite of Sir Eldred's fame among his contemporaries, and Mrs. Montagu's declaration—a very partial one, we must believe, "that The Bleeding Rock will stand, unimpaired by ages, as eminent as any in the Grecian Parnassus;" and of Richard Burke, who calls them "truly elegant and tender performances," we cannot help thinking that the moral embraced in Sir

Eldred's closing lines is destined to a far longer existence, than the legend which verifies it.

> " The deadliest wounds with which we bleed,
>   Our crimes inflict alone ;
> Man's *mercies* from God's hand proceed,
>   His miseries from his own."

Garrick, for so many years the pride of the English stage, was now upon the eve of quitting it forever, in order to taste the sweets, and enjoy the calm of private life. Having nearly reached his " chair age," and becoming subject to severe attacks of sickness, which must soon impair his physical powers, he resolved to leave with all his honors thick upon him. Before doing so, he consented once more, and for the last time, to exhibit those remarkable powers which inspired Dr. Franklin to write at once a correct criticism and just eulogy in the following lines :—

> " So when Great Shakspeare to his Garrick joined,
>   With mutual aid conspire to rouse the mind,
>   'Tis not a scene of idle mimicry ;
>   'Tis Lear's, Hamlet's, Richard's self we see.
>   We feel the actor's strength, the poet's fire ;
>   With joy we praise, with rapture we admire,
>   To see such powers within the reach of art,
>   And fiction thus subdue the human heart."

For two or three weeks, Drury Lane was filled with admiring audiences. In the character of Hamlet, Garrick
is said particularly to have excelled, filling, with singular
power, says one, the whole soul of the spectator, and
transcending the most finished idea of the poet.

" I have, at last," writes Hannah on this occasion to Dr.
Stonehouse, " had the entire satisfaction of seeing Garrick
in Hamlet. Posterity will never be able to form the
slightest idea of his powers. The more I see him, the
more I wonder and admire. It seems to me as if I had
been assisting at the funeral obsequies of the poets. I feel
almost as much pain as pleasure. He is quite happy in
the prospect of his release."

The strong intelligence of his eye, the animated and
ever-varying expression of his whole countenance, the flexibility of his voice, with his grace and ease of attitude, is
said altogether to have produced an indescribable and
profound impression upon the mind, and one which no
language can convey to another.

At the final parting Garrick wept, while tears and applauses accompanied from the stage. This occurred in
May, 1776.

He soon afterwards disposed of his share in Drury Lane
for £35,000, and retreated to domestic privacy, in hope,

perhaps, of spending the last acts of life's drama in scenes
more befitting a final exit behind the curtain of eternity.
Touching the event, Hannah thus expresses herself in the
concluding verses of a little poem, written after her return
to Bristol, and addressed to Dragon, Garrick's favorite dog.

"How wise! long pampered with applause,
To make a voluntary pause,
    And lay his laurels down!
Boldly repelling each strong claim,
To dare assert to wealth and fame,
    Enough of both I've known.

How wise! a short retreat to steal,
The vanity of life to feel,
    And from its cares to fly;
To act one calm, domestic scene,
Earth's bustle and the grave between,
    Retire, and learn to die."

What Dragon failed to appreciate in the ode, the poet
naturally concluded his master would, and it issues from
her pen an utterance of grateful love for the affection and
kindness unsparingly bestowed upon her by his famed
master. Ah, yes, humorously sings the bard,

"I'd get my master's ways by rote,
  Ne'er would I bark at ragged coat,
    Nor tear the tattered sinner;
  Like him, I'd love the dog of merit,
  Caress the cur of broken spirit,
    And give them all a dinner.

And then on me what joys would wait;
  Were I the guardian of the gate,
    How useless bolt and latch!
  How vain were locks, and bars how vain,
  To shield from harm the household train
    Whom I, from love, would watch!"

Manuscript copies of this little poem were handed
around and read by her friends, until she was induced to
publish it in 1778, when a thousand copies were sold in a
single week.

On the following summer we find Miss More journeying
into Norfolk, hunting up old friends of her father, visiting
country cousins, eating brown bread and custards, and
thoroughly appreciating all the good sense which fell in
her way.

Hannah never knew whether to be angry or ashamed,
whether to scold or to blush at the fashionable impositions

of her day. "I protest," she exclaimed, in speaking of some young ladies who came in to pay her an evening's visit, "I hardly do them justice when I pronounce that they had among them, on their heads, an acre and an half of shrubbery, besides slopes, grass-plats, tulip-beds, clumps of peonies, kitchen-gardens, and green-houses."

"Some ladies carry on their heads a large quantity of fruit, and yet they would despise a poor, useful member of society, who carried it there for the purpose of selling it for bread.   Spirit of Addison!" she humorously supplicates— "thou, who with such fine humor and polished sarcasm didst lash the cherry-colored hood and party patches, and cut down a whole harvest of follies, awake! for the follies thou didst lash were but the beginning of follies! and the absurdities thou didst censure were but the seeds of absurdities!"

Garrick, it is said, struck the first blow to this fashionable folly, by appearing one evening on the stage, his cap decorated with a profusion of every sort of vegetable, with a huge carrot hanging down on either side.

One cannot help thinking that the spirit of reform has been heard in the councils of fashion, for her sway is surely less capricious and more benign in our own day; indeed, when we compare the frightful wigs and cushions, the high-heeled shoes and buckram bodices of our grandames, with the comparative ease and naturalness of our own times, one cannot help hoping that Fashion has entered into a league of good fellowship with Nature, graciously allowing her the exercise of some of her inalienable rights to life and liberty, if not to the pursuit of happiness.

But if the follies of London, aped in the retreats of Hertfordshire, pained and provoked her, she found some amends in a visit to Mrs. Barbauld, and in the sterling merits of her cousin Cotton, from whose style of living she draws the following sensible conclusion, true all the world over, and worthy the serious consideration of people whose expenses are getting the better of their principles and their purses. "I have long ago found out, that hardly anybody but frugal, plain people, do generous things. Our cousin Cotton, who, I dare say, is often ridiculed for his simplicity and frugality, could yet lay down £200, without being sure of ever receiving a shil ling interest, for the laudable purpose of establishing a worthy minister, to whom he is still a very considerable contributor. This is commonly the case; and I am apt to conceive a prejudice against everybody who makes a great figure, and to suspect those who *talk* generously."

On her return, she accompanied the Garricks to Farnborough Place, the residence of Mr. Wilmot, where she met, among other distinguished guests, Dr. Kennicott, Hebrew Professor of Oxford, and his wife, with whom Miss More was soon on an intimate footing.

In the year 1777, Miss More again took up her pen, and at the urgent entreaty of Garrick, determined to try her powers in drama. "Percy" was the fruit of her labors. She sent it to him, who, delighted with her success, recommended it to Mr. Harris, the manager of Drury Lane. The tragedy was accepted, and preparations were speedily made for bringing it out. Hannah went down to London to bespeak a prologue from Garrick; for which, on being finished, he humorously begged to know what she meant to pay him;—Dryden, he declared, used to have five guineas, but as he was a richer man, he would be content with a handsome supper. Hannah insisted she could only afford a beef-steak and a bottle of porter; but at last they settled down on toast and honey, —highly flavored, we may venture to add, with wit and good humor.

Percy was received with acclamation, and was played for twelve nights to overflowing houses, netting her £700.

The Duke of Northumberland, and the Earl of Percy, sent to congratulate her on her great success, and to thank her for the honor she had done them, by selecting her subject from the historical records of their family. Detained at home by the gout, they sent and bought tickets, for which they paid as "became the blood of the Percies."

"Many scenes in this play," says Davies, Garrick's biographer, "prognosticate to our stage a rising genius in tragedy, who, in time, will produce scenes, not inferior to the best of Otway and Southem, without that mixture of licentiousness and vulgarity, which disgrace the productions of these writers."

The success of Percy increased the interest already felt in Hannah More by her London friends. She is beset with engagements and visitations. One day we find her at Sir Joshua's, another at Mrs. Montagu's, with Mrs. Chapone, Mrs. Boscawen, and Miss Carter; another at the Garricks', with the "Sour-crout party," a meeting of learned men once a week at dinner, at which sour-crout always made a dish, and to which Miss More was always invited, when she was in town.

"They are playing Percy," writes its author to her sisters, "at this very moment, for the seventh time. I never think of going: it is very odd, but it does not amuse me."

"Last night was the ninth of Percy: it was a brilliant house, and *I* was there. Lady North did me the honor to take a stage-box. I trembled when the wickedness of going to war was spoken, as I was afraid my Lord was in the house, and that speech, though not written with any particular design, is so bold, and is so warmly received, that it frightens me. Mrs. Montagu had a box again; which, as she is a consummate critic, and is hardly ever seen at a public place, is a great credit to the play. We spent an agreeable evening together at Dr. Cadogan's, where she and I, being the only two monsters in the creation, who never touch a card (and laughed at enough we are for it), had the fireside to ourselves; and a more elegant and instructive conversation I have seldom enjoyed. I met Mrs. Chapone one day at Mrs. Montagu's: she is one of Percy's warmest admirers; and as she does not go to plays, but has formed her opinion in the closet, it is more flattering."

"Mrs. Garrick came to me this morning, and wished me to go to the Adelphi, which I declined doing, being so ill. She would have gone herself to fetch me a physician, and insisted upon sending me my dinner, which I refused; but at six this evening, when Garrick came to the Turk's Head to dine, there accompanied him in the coach, a minced chicken in the stew-pan, hot, a canister of her fine tea, and a pot of cream. Were there ever such people? Tell it not in Epic or Lyric, that the great Roscius rode with a stew-pan of minced meat with him in the coach, for my dinner. Percy is acted again this evening; do any of you choose to go? For my own part, I shall enjoy a much superior pleasure—that of sitting by the fire, in a good chair, and being denied to all company: what is Percy to this?"

Miss More remained at London during the winter, and in April, 1778, returned to Bristol, where she spent the summer, in the quiet enjoyment of those pursuits so congenial to her tastes, and in the exercise of those dear, delightful home affections, which made the sunshine of her life.

6*

CHAPTER V.

Death of Garrick—On Theatrical Amusements.

THE New-Year's greetings of 1779 had scarcely died away, before the tidings of Garrick's death startled and saddened the English public. Amid the Christmas festivities of Althorp, whither he had gone with his wife, he had been suddenly stricken by his old complaint, the stone, whose premonitory warnings he had disregarded, in leaving home and mingling at all in the gayeties of the season.

Recovering a little, he was carried to London, where it was thought skill and attention might again restore him. The distemper not yielding to the usual remedies, some of the most able practitioners of the city came unbidden to his bedside; but the power of human science, and the faithful nursing of his wife, availed not. Life was ebbing. His family physician informed him that if he had any worldly affairs to settle, it would be prudent to despatch them as soon as possible.

"I have nothing of that kind to do," answered Garrick, on whose now wan and sunken face, the shadow of death was already passing.

Wednesday morning, January 20th, 1779, witnessed his closing act in the great drama of life.

Obedient to the summons of the afflicted wife, Hannah arose from her sick bed, and with a sorrowing heart, hastened to the house of death. Mrs. Garrick sunk into her arms. "I have this moment embraced his coffin, and you come next!" she exclaimed, with a bursting heart; "the goodness of God to me is inexpressible. I do not deserve it, but I am thankful for it."

What a change in the princely mansion! the wit, the genius, the presence of its "well-graced master," were no longer there. Sorrow sat upon every household face, and the rooms were hung with the drapery of mourning.

After mingling her tears, and ministering her consolations to the living, she paid a melancholy visit to all that was left of the departed.

"His new house," she says, "is not so pleasant as Hampton, or so splendid as the Adelphi, but it is commodious enough for the wants of its inhabitant; and besides, it is so quiet that he will never be disturbed until the eternal morning. May he then find mercy!"

The funeral solemnities took place on the first of February, when his body was borne in all the pomp and circumstance of an English public burial, to Westminster Abbey, and laid in the poet's corner, beneath the tomb of Shakspeare.

Hannah, accompanied by Miss Cadogan, who had gained tickets of admission into the Abbey—no one being allowed an entrance without a passport from the Bishop—sat in a little gallery directly over the grave, where she could distinctly hear and see the solemn ceremony. " And this is all of Garrick," was the sad utterance of her heart— " yet a very little while and he shall say to the worm, Thou art my brother; and to corruption, Thou art my mother and my sister. So passes away the fashion of this world."

For the sake of his friendship for Hannah More, and the discerning appreciation which he seems to have entertained for her abilities, as well as for his wonderful dramatic power, and the amiable and friendly intercourse which we have holden with him in these brief pages, shall we not add a few more words before the final leave-taking?

There may be some, whose inquiries we might anticipate by adding, that David Garrick was born in Litchfield, of respectable parents, in the year 1716. At the age of nineteen, he became a pupil in the newly opened seminary of Samuel Johnson, which, after a few weeks' trial, was abandoned both by pupil and teacher. The two then joined together, determined to push for London, the Mecca of so many pilgrims, the grave of so many hopes. But while many a poet and genius had dropped like untimely fruit from the tree of life, in the foul and murky atmosphere of London, Johnson and Garrick fought their way through every hindrance, which the lack of fortune and of friends may be conceived to set up, and became, at last, among the great men of their times; each, in his own sphere, the greatest that had yet been.

As an actor, Garrick is said never to have had a competitor—never an equal. He won fame, fortune, and friends, while his domestic virtues, ample means, and refined tastes, placed him in a social position far above the men of his profession; and yet must we not add—poor Garrick!

Social life, refined, graceful, thoughtless, was the element in which he lived and moved: his marvellous powers adorned and delighted the world, and the world rewarded her gifted votary. Yet to the sober eye of reason, and the severer decisions of christian requirement, the treasures of his genius were wasted to serve the poor purpose of amusing his fellow-men, and futurity was mortgaged for the gay sunshine of an hour.

The soul, bereaved of its spiritual susceptibilities, and beggared of its heavenly hopes, meets death with calm indifference,

> Were "life but a walking shadow; a poor player
> That struts and frets his hour upon the stage,
> And then is heard no more"—

then were all well—*but after death is the Judgment.*

Miss More, after Garrick's death, wrote two more dramas; "The Fatal Falsehood," and "The Inflexible Captive;" and with these closed her contributions to the stage. This period of intellectual excitement and literary success was brief as it was brilliant; for her views of theatrical amusements had already become modified by an increasing observation of their effects, and a few years later, she came to regard them dangerous to morals, and hostile to christian virtue.

There are few, perhaps, whose opinions upon this subject are more entitled to a respectful hearing, not only because her social connections and friendly intercourse with Garrick would have tempted her to view them in the most favorable light, but because she cannot be accused of any secret or early bias against them, it being thought no robbery of religious character for dignitaries and members of the church to frequent the theatre ; her opinions, therefore, are the candid and impartial result of a clear head and a correct heart.

"Why," let us ask her, " why write for the stage at all ?"

" Because," she replies, " I was led to entertain, what I must now think, a delusive hope that the stage, under certain regulations, might be converted into a school of virtue —that though a bad play would always be a bad thing, yet the representation of a good one might become not only harmless, but useful. On these grounds I attempted some theatrical compositions, which, whatever other defects might be justly imputed to them, should at least have been written on the side of virtue and modesty, and which should neither hold out any corrupt image to the mind or any impure description to the fancy."

Are not then good plays harmless, nay, improving ?

" There will still remain, even in tragedies," she replies, " otherwise the most unexceptionable, provided they are sufficiently impassioned to produce a powerful effect on the feelings, and have spirit enough to deserve to become popular, an essential, radical defect. What I insist on is, that there almost inevitably runs through the whole web of the tragic drama, a prominent thread of false principle. It is generally the leading object of the poet to erect a standard of *honor*, in direct opposition to the standard of Christianity. Worldly honor is the very soul, and spirit, and life-giving principle of the drama. It is her moral and political law. Fear and shame are the capital crimes in her code. Love, jealousy, hatred, ambition, pride, revenge, are too often elevated into the rank of splendid virtues, and form a dazzling system of worldly morality in direct contradiction to the spirit of Christianity. The fruits of the Spirit and the fruits of the stage, if the parallel were followed up, would exhibit as pointed a contrast as human imagination could conceive."

What! must the merits of every play be tried by the Ten Commandments?

" We may at least venture to answer, that they should contain nothing *hostile* to them. If harmless merriment be not expected to *advance* our moral improvement, we must take care that it do not oppose it; for if we concede that our amusements are not expected to make us better than we are, ought we not to be careful that they do not make us worse than they find us? Whatever pleasantry

of idea, or gayety of sentiment we admit, should we not
jealously watch against any unsoundness in the general
principle, or mischief in the prevailing tendency ?"

But what essential difference is there between *reading*
a play and *seeing* it acted ; surely one would not object to
reading dramatic composition ?

"I think there is a substantial difference," she still
argues, "between seeing and reading a dramatic composition, and that the objections which lie so strongly against
the one, are not, at least in the same degree, applicable to
the other. While there is an essential and inseparable
danger attendant on dramatic exhibitions, the danger in
reading a play arises solely from the improper *sentiments*
contained in it. It is the semblance of real action which
is given to the piece by different persons supporting the
different parts, and by their dress, tones, and gestures,
heightening the representation into a kind of enchantment.
It is the pageantry, the splendor of the spectacle, and even
the show of the spectators, these are the circumstances
which fill the theatre, produce the effect, and create the
danger. These give a pernicious force to sentiments,
which, when read, may merely explain the mysterious
action of the human heart, but which, when thus uttered
and accompanied, become contagious and destructive.

7

These, in short, make up a scene of temptation and seduction, of over-wrought voluptuousness and unnerving pleasure, which ill accords with a desire to be enlightened by the doctrines, or governed by the principles of the gospel of Jesus Christ."

But may not the stage become purified, so as to render it at least harmless and unobjectionable?

"What the stage might be under another and an imaginary state of things, it is not very easy for us to know, and therefore, not very important to inquire. Nor is it the soundest logic to argue on the possible goodness of a thing, which, in the present circumstances of society, is doing positive evil, from the imagined good that thing might be conjectured to produce in a supposed state of unattainable improvement; for unfortunately nothing can be done until not only the stage itself has undergone complete purification, but until the audience shall be purified also. We must first suppose a state of society in which the spectators will be disposed to relish all that is pure, and to reprobate all that is corrupt, before the system of a pure and uncorrupt theatre can be adopted with any reasonable hope of success; there must always be a harmony between the taste of the spectator and the nature of the spectacle, in order to produce pleasure, for people go to a play not to be instructed, but to be amused."

Let every thoughtful parent, doubting Christian, or tempted youth, read carefully, and ponder seriously these positions. There is, perhaps, no question in christian education more difficult to settle than what amusements are safe for our children, or what recreations the young Christian, away from the restraints and pastimes of home, may engage in with safety to himself and honor to his Divine Master.

We would point the latter to those principles laid down to Wesley by his mother : " Whatever weakens your reason, impairs the tenderness of your conscience, obscures your sense of God, or takes off the relish of spiritual things, —in short, whatever increases the strength and authority of your body over your mind, that thing is *sin* to you, however innocent it may be in itself."

And yet you may be placed amid influences, which, for a time, may blind your judgment, and persuade you from your steadfastness : you find yourself overpowered by plausible reasoning, which you cannot readily meet, and because you cannot meet it, you are tempted to yield. You are not unlikely to find yourself thus perplexed : what shall you do? Shall you yield without hearty conviction, in deference merely to the skill or sneer of your companions?

What shall you do? Refer *to the example of intelligent men and women, eminent for holiness :* how *have devoted servants of God viewed the subject ?* What has been the christian apprehension of the church upon the matter? It is of no great consequence whether you understand or not the train of thought or course of argument by which their minds were made up and their conduct directed ; you have no time, it may be, to examine them if you would ; it is enough to know how they acted, and that it will be safe and wise to imitate their example.

Do not hesitate to lean upon an argument like this, in harmony with the spirit of the Word of God. It is no sign of weakness to take counsel of the matured judgments of christian experience, or of growth and manliness to disregard them.

CHAPTER VI.

Correspondence.

"I WISH you a merry Christmas as well as a happy New Year, but that I hate the word merry as so applied; it is a fitter epithet for a bacchanalian than a christian festival, and seems an apology for idle mirth and injurious excess. What frost! what snow! The vast expanse of glittering white on the ground, the fluid brilliants dropping from the trees, and the green-house full of beautiful blossoms and oranges, make it altogether look like some region of enchantment; and as the gravel walks are all swept clean, I parade an hour or two every morning."

1781.

"If I commit any sin here or do any good here, it must be in thought, for our words are few and our deeds not at all. Poor Hermes Harris is dead! Everybody is dead, I think—one is almost ashamed of being alive! That you may not think I pass my time quite idly, I must tell you

7*

that I had begun Belshazzar; I like the subject, and have made some progress in it. But that and all my other occupations have given way to the melancholy employment of reading over with Mrs. Garrick all the private letters of the dear deceased master of this melancholy mansion. The employment, though sad, is not without its amusement; it is reading the friendly correspondence of all the men who have made a figure in the annals of business or of literature for the last forty years; for I think I hardly miss a name of eminence in Great Britain, and not many in France; it includes also all his answers, some of the first wits in the country confessing their obligations over and over again to his bounty; money given to some, and lent to such numbers as would be incredible if one did not read it in their own letters. It is not the least instructive part of this employment to consider where almost all these great men are now! the play-writers, where are they? and the poets, are their fires extinguished? Did Lord Bath, or Bishop Warburton, or Lord Chatham, or Goldsmith, or Churchill, or Chesterfield, trouble themselves with thinking that the heads that dictated those bright epistles would so soon be laid low? Did they imagine that such a nobody as I am, whom they would have disdained to

have reckoned ' with the dogs of their flock,' should have
had the arranging and disposing of them ?"

LONDON, April, 1781.

" I was last Monday at a meeting at the Bishop of St.
Asaphs, and had the pleasure of a vast deal of snug chat
with the Bishop, Mr. Walpole, Mrs. Montagu, and Mrs.
Carter.

Mrs. Kennicott tells me Bishop Lowth insists upon my
publishing " Sensibility," and all my other poems together,
immediately, that people may have them all together.
The Dean of Gloucester has sent me his book against
Locke, splendidly bound.

On Friday I dined at Mrs. Boscawen's. We had a
snug day and a deal of that social, cordial chat that is so
preferable to all the mummery of great parties.

Tuesday we were a small and choice party at Bishop
Shipley's. Lord and Lady Spencer, Lord and Lady Al-
thorpe, Sir Joshua, Boswell, Gibbon, and to my agreeable
surprise, Dr. Johnson.

Mrs. Garrick and he had never met since her bereavement. Johnson came to see us the next morning, and
made us a long visit. On Mrs. Garrick's telling him she
was always more at ease with persons who had suffered

the same loss with herself, he said that was a comfort she
could seldom have, considering the superiority of his meri.
and the cordiality of their union.   He bore his strong testimony of the liberality of Garrick.   He reproved me with
pretended sharpness for reading Pascal or any of the Por-
Royal authors, alleging, that as a good Protestant, I ough
to abstain from books written by Catholics.   I was begin
ning to stand upon my defence, when he took me with
both hands, and with a tear running down his cheeks
' Child,' said he, with the most affecting earnestness, '
am heartily glad that you read pious books, by whomso-
ever they may be written.' "

"On Monday we had a farewell party at Mrs. Vesey's
where we were a little sad to think how many of us migh
never meet again, particularly poor Mrs. Vesey herself
who is going to Ireland at an advanced age, and in bad
health."

"On Tuesday, Mrs. Boscawen carried me to Glanvilla;
we had the pleasantest tête-à-tête day imaginable, and
walked about and sat under the spreading oak, and eat
our cold chicken, and drank our tea, as happy folks are
wont to do."

In June, Miss More returned to her sisters, taking Mrs.

Garrick with her, who remained a month at Bristol. Hannah stayed until December, wnen she again took u her abode in her friend's family.

Sensibility, a short poem, which a good critic of our own day declares " should be printed in letters of gold," had been passed around in manuscript among her friends, at whose repeated and urgent request it was now published, in company with four sacred dramas. The poem was addressed to her friend, Mrs. Boscawen, and thus gracefully opens :—

> " Accept, Boscawan ! these unpolished lays,
>   Nor blame too much the verse you cannot praise.
>   For you far other bards have waked the string,
>   Far other bards for you were wont to sing :
>   Yet on the gale their parting music steals,
>   Yet your charmed ear the lov'd impression feels ;
>   You hear the lyres of Littleton and Young,
>   And this a grace and that a seraph strung."

" What says my dear Miss More ?" writes she, from Glan villa, on learning that her name was in the golden touch of the poet ; " that she has addressed her charming poem of ' Sensibility' to one who has not a grain of that pleasing, painful quality ; and that, if she ever writes upon stupidity, she will with more propriety direct to the same quarter."

And still later. "They are come out! the books I mean; I have found them just now in the hall, a packet from Mr. Cadell: I had them brought up. 'I put in my thumb and pulled out a plumb:' viz., I drew out one all sewed in yellow, as I directed, and while Ayre is carefully cutting the leaves, I sit down to write to the founder of the feast."

On the feast the founder herself writes to her sisters—

"The word *sacred* in the title is a damper in the dramas. It is tying a mill-stone about the neck of Sensibility, which will drown them both together. I was one night at a large Blue Stocking party, at the Bishop of St. Asaph's—all the old set were there, which sickness and death have spared.

"Bishop Lowth has just finished the Dramas, and sent me word, that although I have paid him the most swinging compliment he ever received, he likes the whole book more than he can say. But the Bishop of Chester's compliment is more solid; he said he thought it would do a vast deal of *good*—and that is the praise best worth having."

" Mrs. Montagu, Chapone, and Carter, are mightily

pleased, that I have attacked that mock feeling and sensibility, which is at once the boast and disgrace of these times, and which is equally deficient in taste and truth. Ask Dr. Stonehouse if he has read " Cardiphonia," by Mr. Newton, of Olney. There is in it much vital religion, and much of the experience of a good Christian, who feels and laments his own imperfections and weaknesses. I have just finished six volumes of Jortin's sermons; elegant, but cold and very low in doctrine—'plays round the head, but comes not to the heart'—Cardiphonia does; I like it much, though not every sentiment or expression that it contains."

"On Monday, I was at a very great assembly at the Bishop of St. Asaph's. Conceive to yourself one hundred and fifty to two hundred people met together, dressed in the extremity of fashion; painted as red as bacchanals; poisoning the air with perfumes; treading on each other's gowns; making the crowd they blame; not one in ten able to get a chair; protesting they are engaged to ten other places, and lamenting the fatigue they are not obliged to endure; ten or a dozen card-tables crammed with dowagers of quality, grave ecclesiastics, and yellow admirals; and you have an idea of an assembly. I never go to such things when I can possibly avoid it, and stay, when there, as few minutes as I can."

LONDON, 1782.

"Poor Johnson is in quite a bad state of health: I fear his constitution is broken up; I am quite grieved at it; he will not leave an abler defender of religion and virtue behind him, and the following little touch of tenderness which I heard of him last night from one of the Turk's Head Club, endears him to me exceedingly. There are always a great many candidates ready, when any vacancy happens in that club, and it requires no small interest and reputation to get elected; but, upon Garrick's death, when numberless applications were made to succeed him, Johnson was deaf to them all; he insisted there should be a year's widowhood in the club before they thought of any new election. In Dr. Johnson some contrarieties harmoniously meet; if he has too little charity for the opinions of others, and too little patience with their faults, he has the greatest tenderness for their persons. He told me, the other day, he hated to hear people whine about metaphysical distresses, when there were so much want and hunger in the world."

"Mrs. Carter and I met at a little breakfast-party with

a French lady, who writes metaphysical books. We got into disgrace by saying that a little common sense and a little scripture would lead one much farther and safer than volumes of metaphysics. She forgave us, however, on condition we would read two huge quartos which she had just translated. What Mrs. Carter will do, I know not, but I shall certainly never fulfil my part of the contract."

In June Hannah makes a summer flitting to the Kennicott's, at Oxford, where she met Dr. Johnson, sad, sick, and disconsolate, suffering deeply from the manifold infirmities of life.

The death of his friend, Mr. Thrale, which had occurred the year before, whose generous hospitality had cheered his heart and alleviated his sufferings, and whose eye for fifteen years, as Johnson tenderly says, "had scarcely been turned upon him, but with respect and tenderness," had left a void, which even the multiplied resources of his inner and outer life had failed to fill up; "and such another friend, the general course of human things will not suffer man to hope," he mournfully adds, "In our walk through life, we have dropped our companions, and are now to pick up such as chance may offer to us, or travel alone. As the long shadows of age and ill health crept over his path, Dr. Johnson felt the want of those home affections, which are

8

our best earthly heritage, and which, when the busy interests of early and middle life are over, bear us gently and patiently in their bosom to our final rest.

In a journey to Oxford, at this time, undertaken for the benefit of his health and spirits, the Doctor met Miss More, who, grieved at his wan and dejected appearance, made every effort to beguile him from his sufferings. The memory of early days quickened the old man eloquent. As in her company he retraced the haunts of his college companions; on entering a hall, a fine large print of Johnson, handsomely framed, stared upon the party from the opposite wall, with the appended motto,

"AND IS NOT JOHNSON OURS, HIMSELF A HOST?"
[From Miss More's Sensibility.]

A pleasing surprise prepared by Dr. Adams, Master of Pembroke, for his distinguished guests.

The Doctor remained but a short time; a few beams from the light of early years shot across his path, but they could not renew the warm hopes of youth, or lighten the infirmities of age.

LONDON, March, 1783.

"On Friday I was at a very fine party at Lady Rothes', where I found a vast many of my friends—Mrs. Montagu,

Boscawen, Carter, Thrall, Burney, and Lady Dartry; in short, it was remarked that there was not a woman in London, who has been distinguished for taste and literature, that was absent. The men were modest and were abashed, the other sex made so strong a party."

"I should be glad to know what our friend Dr. Stonehouse would say to such new-fashioned doctrines as I have lately heard in a charity sermon by a dignified ecclesiastic, and a popular one too, but I will not tell his name: he told the rich and great that they ought to be extremely liberal in their charities, because they were happily *exempted* from the *severer virtues*. How do you like such a sentiment from a christian teacher? What do you think Polycarp or Ignatius would say to it?"

March 27.

"I went and sat the other morning with Dr. Johnson, who is far from well. Our conversation was very interesting, but so many came in that I began to feel foolish, and soon sneaked off."

May 5th.

"Saturday we had a dinner at home, Mrs. Carter, Miss Hamilton, the Kennicotts, and Dr. Johnson. Poor Johnson exerted himself exceedingly, but he was very ill, and

looked so dreadfully, it quite grieved me. His sickness
seems to have softened his mind, without at all weakening
it. We had but a small party of such of his friends as we
knew would be most agreeable to him ; and as we were all
very attentive, and paid him the homage he both expects
and deserves, he was very communicative, and of course
instructive and delightful in the highest degree."

May 22.

"A visitor is just gone, quite chagrined that I am such
a rigid Methodist, that I cannot come to her assembly on
Sunday, though she protests with great piety, that she
never has cards, and that it is quite savage in me to think
there can be any harm in a little agreeable music."

While Hannah was at her sisters' in Bristol, during 1784,
she became greatly interested for a poor woman in the
neighborhood, who, from the depth of famine and distress,
had exhibited striking poetic talent. On a minute inquiry
into her situation, it was ascertained that she could only
read and write. Paradise Lost, Young's Night Thoughts,
a few plays of Shakspeare, and the Bible, constituted her
small stock of reading. Having given her some rules in
the art of writing, Hannah encouraged her to prepare a
small volume of poems, to aid in the support of a family

dependent upon her exertions. The work having been completed, she enlisted her friends in its publication. "I should have taken as much pain as pleasure in the fine stanzas you sent me," responds Mrs. Montagu, "if you had not at the same time assured me you had taken care this noble creature should not want the little comforts of life. I shall most joyfully contribute towards procuring them for her—far, far away, all heathen ethics and mythology, geometry, and algebra, and make room for the Bible and Milton, when a poet is to be made."

Nearly £500 were raised upon the book, which were placed in the hands of trustees, and invested in the public funds for the use of herself and family : enraged that the sum was not placed at her own disposal, she turned against her benefactor with the utmost bitterness of spirit, and accused her of having embezzled it. So outrageous was her conduct, that no one would hold the trust, and the money fell into her own hands, only to be idly squandered, and she died *at last*, destitute and friendless. Of her ingratitude, Hannah writes to Miss Carter : "I grieve for poor fallen human nature ; for as to my own particular part, I am persuaded Providence intends me good by it. Had she turned out well, I should have had my *reward ;* as it is, I have my *trial.* Perhaps I was too vain of my

8*

success, and in counting over the money, might be elated and think—Is not this great Babylon that *I* have built ?"

Two little poems which had been passed around among her friends in manuscript, were now published, The Bas Bleu and Florio. Florio, a pleasing satire on men and manners, was dedicated to Horace Walpole : " It is a paltry return," she writes to him, " for the many hours of agreeable information and elegant amusement which I have received from your spirited and very entertaining writings, and yet I am persuaded you will receive it with favor, as a small offering of esteem and gratitude."

The Bas Bleu, a little poem, already mentioned, commemorative of the gatherings which bore that name, was addressed to Mrs. Vesey, whose celebrated tact in breaking up the formality of a circle, and making her parties form themselves into little groups, is thus sung in poetic numbers :

> "Small were that art which could ensure
> The circle's boasted quadrature !
> See Vesey's plastic genius make
> A circle every figure take ;
> Nay, shapes and forms that would defy
> All science of geometry ;

Isosceles and parallel,

Names hard to speak and hard to spell;

The enchantress waved her wand and spoke !

Her potent wand the circle broke;

The social spirits hover round,

And bless the liberated ground.

Ask you what charms this gift dispense ?

'Tis the strong spell of common sense.

Away dull ceremony flew,

And with her bore Detraction too."

Another of Miss More's friends, and one of the world's great men, was now drawing near to the grave. " Poor, dear Johnson," she writes, " is past all hope. I have, however, the comfort to hear that his dread of dying is in a great measure subdued. He sent the other day for Sir Joshua, and after much serious conversation, told him he had three favors to beg of him, and he hoped he would not refuse a dying friend, be they what they would. Sir Joshua promised. The first was, that he would never paint on Sunday: the second, that he would give him £30 that he had lent him, as he wanted to leave them to a distressed family : the third, that he would read the Bible whenever he had an opportunity, and that he would never omit it on Sunday."

How august and solemn are the closing scenes of this dying man! He is styled the Moralist. Justice, truth, virtue—rough, unhewn, without chisel or polish,—were the pillars of his character; at all times, and in all places, he was loyal to his convictions of duty, generous, yet plain-spoken to his fellows, reverent towards God. Rich in knowledge, he abused it not; rich in thought, he scattered its treasures like dew-drops; rich in speech, it was like the golden harvest: in the wide grasp of his clear, calm, comprehensive mind, he everywhere discovered a moral government, and recognized a righteous governor: his conscience, unseared by passion or self-indulgence, spoke solemnly, and was heard: the fear of God was upon him: but now, as the curtains of death close around his brave heart and unclouded intellect, he lies helpless, wrestling for hope, panting for peace, raising his eyes with a fearful looking for of judgment into the eternal world. "The approach of death is dreadful," he exclaims. "I am afraid to think on that which I know I cannot avoid. It is vain to look round and round for that help which cannot be had, yet we hope and hope, and fancy that he who has lived to-day, may live to-morrow. No wise man will be contented to die, if he thinks he is going into a state of punishment. Nay, no wise man will be contented to die if he thinks he is to fall into annihilation; for, however unhappy any man's existence may be, yet he would rather have it than not exist at all. No: there is no rational principle by which a man can die contented, but a trust in the mercy of God, through the merits of Jesus Christ."

And yet, when one said to him in an hour of gloomy despondency, "you forget the merits of your Redeemer," he replied with deep solemnity, "I do not forget the merits of my Redeemer, but my Redeemer has said, *He will set some on his right hand and some on his left.*"

"What man," he asks, with mournful distrust, "can say that his obedience has been such as he could approve of in another, or that his repentance has not been such as to require being repented of ?"

"Remember what you have done by your writings in defence of virtue and truth," urged his friends.

"Admitting all you say to be true," answered the dying hero, "how can I tell when *I have done enough ?*"

An awful question, who can answer it?

At last, he described the kind of clergyman whom he wished to see. Mr. Winstanley was named, and a note was despatched requesting his attendance to the sick man's chamber. Through ill-health and nervous apprehension, the clergyman could reply only in writing. "Permit me, therefore," ran the note, "to write what I should wish to say, were I present. I can easily conceive what would be the subjects of your inquiry. I can conceive that the views of yourself have changed with your condition, and that on the near approach of death, what you considered mere peccadilloes, have risen into mountains of guilt, while your best actions have dwindled into nothing. On whichever side you look, you see only positive transgression, or defective obedience; and hence, in self-despair, are eagerly asking, ' What shall I do to be saved ?' I say to you in the language of the Baptist, ' Behold the Lamb of God.' "

"Does he say so ?" exclaimed the anxious listener. " Read it again, Sir John." Upon the second reading, Dr. Johnson declared, " I must see that man, write again to him."

A second letter was the reply, enlarging and enforcing upon the subject of the first: " These, together with the conversation of a pious friend, Mr. Latrobe, appear to have been blessed of God," continues one in a letter to Hannah More, " in bringing this great man to a renunciation of self, and a simple reliance on Jesus as his Saviour; thus also communicating to him that peace which he had found the world could not give, and which, when the world was fading from his view, was to fill the void, and dissipate the gloom even of the valley of the shadow of death. The man whose intellectual powers had awed all around him, was in turn made to tremble, when the period arrived, when all knowledge is useless and vanishes away, except the knowledge of the true God and of Jesus Christ whom he has sent. To attain this knowledge, this giant in knowledge must become a little child. The man looked up to as a prodigy of wisdom, must become a fool, that he might be wise."

"For some time before his death, all his fears were calmed and absorbed by the prevalence of his faith and his trust in the merit and propitiation of Jesus Christ," testifies Dr. Brocklesby.

"My dear doctor, believe a dying man," exclaimed Johnson, "there is no salvation but in the Lamb of God."

"How delighted should I be," said Hannah More, "to hear the dying discourse of this great and good man, especially now that faith has subdued his fears."

What teaching is here! No amount of outward obedience, neither gift of mind nor greatness of character, neither fair fame nor good works, quench the restless fears and distressing doubts which fill the heart, when earthly objects begin to fade before eternal realities. The shrinking soul dares not trust itself; those things in which it delighted—

the old walls and familiar haunts, the green earth and pleasant sunshine, the strong limbs and kindly warmth of neighbors and friends, well-earned fame, and hard-wrought achievements, the well-known and dearly-cherished environment of its earthly tabernacle is passing away : passing away, and what is left but the conscious burden of frailty, of short-coming, of guilt. If the soul, thus abased and abandoned, becomes lowly and trusting as the little child, it hears the gracious pleading of its Saviour, " Come unto me, weary and heavy-laden one, and I will give you rest. I am the way, the truth, and the life." Then appear the perfectness and sufficiency of redeeming love. " Except ye be converted and become as a little child, ye cannot enter the kingdom of God."

"The loftiness of man shall be bowed down, and the haughtiness of man shall be laid low, and the Lord alone shall be exalted in that day."

CHAPTER VII.

Cowslip Green.

HITHERTO, Miss More had had many haunts; she **had**
dwelt in the hearts, and by the hearths of many well-
beloved friends : sometimes we find her at Sandleford
Priory, the country retreat of Mrs. Montagu, whose neighborhood abounded with the most smiling valleys, the
clearest living streams, and the most lovely hanging woods
imaginable,—so says the guest : her winters were chiefly
passed between the Adelphi and Hampton, which is "so
clean, so green, so flowery, so bowery :" sometimes she is
brushing the dust off the blue stockings at a splendid dinner at Strafford Place, or at a quiet evening at Berkley
Square, with no other company but "dear Mrs. Carter ;"
lastly, she is nestling with the sisterhood at Bristol. This
changeful and desultory life, as it seems to be, was neither
aimless nor unimproved ; though Miss More had now
nearly reached her fortieth year, and as yet had produced
little but a few poems, whose chief attractions were their

9

ıocal and personal interest, she had not looked idly or too
fondly on the diversified scenes of men and manners passing around her; from these ample opportunities of understanding the moral defects of English society, she was
marshalling her facts and strengthening those principles
which enabled her afterwards to speak so powerfully and
successfully in the parlors and palaces of England.

The death of Garrick had deeply impressed her earnest
and thoughtful mind. It made an abrupt and solemn
pause in her social and intellectual enjoyments. His
taste and genius, his sympathy and interest, delighted and
dazzled her. Her literary tastes were banqueted; the
amplest opportunities to enlarge and cultivate her powers,
were placed at her disposal, and more than all, she is encouraged by one so gifted in the drama, to enter that field
of literature, towards which she seems to have had a
strong and early bias: nay, she had entered the lists, and
Percy had been crowned with laurels.

Garrick died; it was the first death in the brilliant
circle which had first welcomed her to London, and it left
a void never to be filled. In the long shadow which it
cast over his home and haunts, Hannah sat and thought.
She saw the fashion of the world, with its pomps and
praises, passing away   Could these satisfy the hungerings

of the soul? What was that greater good, worthy of the
consecrated energies of the whole heart? She felt deep
within her, that it was not *all* of life to live, nor *all* of
death to die : a conviction that life had a wider sphere,
nobler motives, higher aims, and more exalted hopes, than
literary ambition or intellectual enjoyments could impart,
fastened itself upon her. She saw *accountability to God*,
written as with a pen of fire upon her time and talents.
In the devout solitude of her closet, her solemnized spirit
holds communion with eternal realities ; all earthly things
seem paltry and worthless, compared with the favor of
God ; she inquires, with serious earnestness, what is essential to duty and acceptance in Jesus Christ ; what are
the laws of holy living prescribed in his gospel ; how can
the authority of conscience be maintained amid the conflicts of passion, of sense, and of worldly engagements ;
how run the christian race ; how win the heavenly prize ?
The higher life of the soul began to dawn upon her.

"I have naturally a small appetite for grandeur," she
says, " which is always satisfied, even to indigestion, before
I leave town, and I require a long abstinence to get any
relish for it again ; yet, I repeat, there are very agreeable
people, but, there is dress, there is restraint, there is want

of leisure, to which I find it more difficult to conform for any length of time—and *life is short.*"

One thing which greatly aided her in maintaining an habitual thoughtfulness of mind, amid the giddy disregard of sacred things in much of the society in which she mixed, was her *strict observance of holy time.* The Sabbath was always to her a day of rest; rest from society, from visiting, from all worldly occupations and engagements : she used it, as designed to be used by its great author, a day of religious improvement, a means of holy living, sacred to God and eternal things. Wherever she was, in whatever company she happened to be, she was never afraid of appearing singular, singular as it often did appear, by a devout and respectful observance of the Lord's day.

"You know I often told you," she wrote home, while a resident at the Adelphi, " that Sunday is not only my day of rest, but enjoyment; I go twice to the churches where I expect the best preaching, frequently at St. Clement's, to hear my excellent friend Burrows. Mrs. Garrick declines asking company on Sunday on my account, so that I enjoy the whole day to myself. After my more select reading, I attack South, Atterbury, and Warburton. In these great geniuses and original thinkers, I see many passages of Scripture presented in a strong and striking light. I think

it right to mix their learned labors with the devout effu-
sions of more spiritual writers, Baxter, Doddridge, Hop-
kins, Jeremy Taylor (the Shakspeare of divinity), and the
profound Barrow in turn. I devour much, but I fear
digest little. In the evening, I read a sermon and prayers
to the family, which Mrs. Garrick likes much."

Miss More had for some time gradually contracted her
circle of acquaintance, confining her visits to smaller assemblies and choicer friends.

"I have kept my resolution," she says, "to avoid great
crowds, except when I have been snared into one, under
the alluring name of a little private party, into which trap
I have fallen several times. On Saturday I got a sober
day at Mrs. Montagu's, with only the Smelts', and we all
agreed we had not been more comfortable for a long time;
and yet people rarely have the sense or courage to do
these things, but must still meet in herds and flocks."

She now began to yearn for a home of her own, where
she could enjoy undisturbed retirement, hedged in from
the great world, to pursue her course of thought, of reading, and of occupation, more in harmony with the natural
simplicity of her tastes, and the progressive development of
her religious character. When her purpose of doing so
became known, the notion was assailed by ridicule and

reasoning, and not a few agreed in her speedy and permanent return to London and Bristol.

In spite of forebodings and dissuasives, Miss More, at length, fixed upon a small establishment in the parish of Wrington, ten miles from Bristol, and so secluded from the hum of the great world as to be unvisited even by the post. Here is a thatched roof cottage, the prettiest little hermitage that can be ; flowers edge the walks and fringe the green lawn, which slopes gently towards the south, diversified by groups of shrubbery here and there, tastefully arranged, pleasing to the eye, and affording a refreshing shade from the noon-tide heats. Beyond, in the dusky distance, rises the Mendip Ridge, bold and grand. Behold Cowslip Green; Horace Walpole calls it a cousin to Strawberry-Hill—a country cousin, one fancies.

"I am fitting up a tiny boudoir at Cowslip Green," says the new mistress of the cottage, "which I intend shall contain no literature but the offerings of kindness : by this means, my imagination will convert my little closet into a temple of friendship ; and when the weather is bad, or my spirits low, what a cordial it will be to fancy that I am loved and esteemed by so many amiable and worthy people as there have contributed to my instruction and delight !"

"What book shall I send?" asks Mr. Pepys, one of her friends and favorites. "To send you a skimming-dish or fish-kettle towards setting up house-keeping would be making too little distinction between you and the next good housewife in the parish; but if you would be so good as to tell me any pleasant companion, who is not already of your party, I should have particular pleasure in sending him, and should be very much flattered with the idea, that on some lonely evening he might recall me to your memory."

"I am mightily at a loss," she humorously replies, "what book you will send. What think you of a cook-book? No! that won't do either, for it will introduce sauces and luxury, and all manner of cunningly devised dishes, and extravagant inventions into a little cottage devoted to simplicity, and from which aspiring thoughts and luxurious desires are to be entirely excluded. I should beg a wooden dish and maple spoon, but that it is pleasanter to one's friends to be remembered in one's more intellectual hours. Pray take notice, it must not be a *fine, new book*, out of the shop; that would destroy the charm, which lies in this, that the book must be transplanted from the library of a friend."

She afterwards wrote to the same gentleman: "After

living melodious days with Mrs. Montagu, the nightingales
and Spenser, I have now been quietly set down in my cottage a month, and the evil days have not come, wherein
you barbarously prophesied that I should feel a joy even
to see the apothecary ride up to the door,—though it is
certain I never *do* see him without thinking of you. I do
not express myself very accurately when I talk of living
quietly; for, in truth, my neighbors are so kind, and so
many people have brought themselves into the description,
that I am far from enjoying that perfect retreat, which I
had figured to myself. I work in my garden all the morning, and ride in the evening through delicious lanes and
hills: my most serious studies have been a little book of
Mrs. Trimmer's, that wise and pleasant friend of little children,—it is a most delectable history of Robin Red-
Breast."

In relation to the temptations which clogged her
spiritual progress, and disquieted her spirit in the new
home which she had chosen, she thus expresses herself, to
Rev. John Newton :—

"The care of my garden gives me employment, health,
and spirits. I want to know, dear sir, if it is peculiar to
myself to form ideal plants of perfect virtue, and to dream
of all manner of imaginary goodness in untried circum-

stances, while one neglects the immediate duties of one's actual situation? Do I make myself understood? I have always fancied, that if I could secure to myself such a quiet retreat as I have now really accomplished, I should be wonderfully good; that I should have leisure to store my mind with such and such maxims of wisdom; that I should be safe from such and such temptations; that, in short, my whole summers would be smooth periods of peace and goodness. Now the misfortune is, I have actually found a great deal of the comfort I expected, but without any of the concomitant virtues. I am certainly happier here than in the agitation of the world, but I do not find that I am one bit better; with full *leisure* to rectify my heart and affections, the disposition unluckily does not come. I have the mortification to find that petty and (as they are called) innocent employments can detain my heart from heaven as much as tumultuous pleasures. If to the pure all things are pure, the reverse must be also true, when I can contrive to make so harmless an employment as the cultivation of flowers stand in the room of a vice, by the great portion of time I give up to it, and by the entire dominion it has over my mind. You will tell me that if the affections be estranged from their proper object, it signifies not much whether a bunch of roses or a

pack of cards affects it. I pass my life in intending to get
the better of this, but life is passing away, and the reform
never begins. It is a very significant saying, though a
very old one, of one of the Puritans, that 'hell is paved
with good intentions!' I sometimes tremble to think
how large a square my procrastination alone may furnish
to this tesselated pavement."

"What you are pleased to say, my dear madam, of
the state of your mind, I understand perfectly well," answers this good man, who well understood the deceitfulness of the human heart; "I praise God on your behalf,
and I hope I shall earnestly pray for you. I have stood
upon that ground myself.

"We are apt to wonder that, when what we accounted
hindrances are removed, and the things which we conceived would be great advantages are put within our
power, still there is a secret something in the way, which
proves itself to be independent of all external changes,
because it is not affected by them. The disorder we com-
plain of is internal; and in allusion to our Lord's words
upon another occasion, I may say, it is *not anything in
our outward situation* (provided it be not actually unlaw-
ful) that can *prevent or even retard our advances* in re-

ligion ; we are defiled and impeded by that which is within. So far as our hearts are right, all places and circumstances which this wise and good providence allots us are nearly equal : their hindrances will prove helps ; losses, gains ; and crosses will ripen into comforts ; but till we are so far apprized of the nature of our disease as to put ourselves into the hands of the great and only Physician, we shall find, like the woman in Luke viii. 43, that every other effort for relief will leave us as it found us.

" Our first thought when we begin to be displeased with ourselves, and sensible that we have been wrong, is to attempt to reform ; to be sorry for what is amiss, and to endeavor to amend. It seems reasonable to ask, what can we do more? but while we think we can do so much as this, we do not fully understand the design of the gospel. This gracious message from the God who knows our frame speaks home to our case. It treats us as sinners—as those who have already broken the original law of our nature, in departing from God our creator, supreme lawgiver, and benefactor, and of having lived to ourselves instead of devoting all our time, talents, and influence to his glory. As sinners, the first things we need are pardon, reconciliation and a principle of life and conduct entirely new.

" For these purposes we are directed to Jesus Christ, as
the wounded Israelites were to look at the brazen serpent.
John iii. 14, 15. When we understand what the Scripture teaches of the person, love, and offices of Christ, the
necessity and final cause of his humiliation unto death,
and feel our own need of such a Saviour, we then know
him to be the light, the sun of the world and of the soul ;
the source of all spiritual light, life, comfort, and influence ;
having access by God to him, and receiving out of his
fulness grace for grace.

" Our perceptions of these things are for a time faint and
indistinct, like the peep of dawn; but the dawning light,
though faint, is the sure harbinger of approaching day.

" The beginnings of spiritual life are small in the true
Christian ; *he* passes through a succession of various dispensations, but he advances, though silently and slowly,
yet surely, and will stand forever.

" At the same time, it must be admitted that the christian life is a warfare. Much within us and much without
us must be resisted. In such a world as this, and with
such a nature as *ours*, there will be a call for habitual
self-denial. We must learn to cease from depending
upon our own supposed wisdom, power, and goodness, and

from self-complacency and self-seeking, that we may rely upon Him whose wisdom and power are infinite."

What individual, earnestly striving for a better life, has not sighed over the clogs and hindrances which beset his path, and which he fondly imagines other situations are exempt from; were this wish fulfilled, were that place attained, another goal reached, this obstacle removed, then how easy the yoke, how light the burden, how smooth the way! Alas, no! no situation is free from straits and perplexities, nowhere are we exempt from the necessity of watchfulness and combat. The evil is within us. "The things that we would, we do not, and the things that we would not, those we do." "The flesh lusteth against the spirit, and the spirit against the flesh, and these are contrary the one to the other." In this perpetual conflict how can the victory be secured? Only by watchfulness and prayer through our Lord Jesus Christ.

10

CHAPTER VIII.

FROM the time that Cowslip Green became her home in 1785, may be dated higher views of duty, a more confirmed religious character and a clearer comprehension of her sphere of usefulness. As the retreat was not sought for day-dreaming leisure, her time was not whiled away in literary effeminacy, or her pen consecrated to fairy fancies or pleasing fictions. Hannah More soon found she had a work to do for the day and generation in which she lived, and she wrought courageously, patiently, and with a full heart.

The first fruit of Cowslip Green was a small work, entitled, " Thoughts on the Importance of the Manners of the Great to General Society," an introductory chapter, as it were, to that elevated series of christian teaching, which her life and writings hereafter developed.

It first appeared anonymously, " not so much for the fear of man," she says, " which worketh a snare, as because, if anonymous, it may be ascribed to some better person, and because I fear I do not live as I write. I hope it may be useful to myself, at least as I give a sort of public pledge of my principles, to which I pray, I may be enabled to act up."

It was at first attributed to Wilberforce, then to the Bishop of London. While the author was yet unknown, the book being canvassed in her presence, she was abruptly asked, if she could conjecture who he could be. "Whoever the author may be, I doubt not the writer was in earnest," replied Miss More, with the utmost self-possession. But the authorship did not long remain a secret; while still in London, whither she had gone to superintend its publication, she received an anonymous epigram,

"Of sense and religion in this little book,
All agree there's a wonderful store;
But while round the world for an author they look,
I only am wishing for *More*."

This was her first attack upon the unchristian habits and minor immoralities of the age : her long and intimate acquaintance with the higher ranks of English society, for whom as the title indicates the book was expressly written, enabled her to write with truth and directness : she knew

whereof she spake—"yet I have not gone deep," she
says, "it is confined to prevailing practical evils—should
this succeed, I hope by the blessing of God to attack the
principle." Rev. John Newton congratulates her upon
the performance and especially the choice of a subject;
and it is a subject most admirably handled. She describes,
with great clearness, the features and influence of that
large class of negative characters, abounding in . every
community, which may be called *good sort of people ;*
people, who live within the restraints of moral obligation
and acknowledge the truth of the christian religion, yet
whose views terminate with this world's good, who are
destitute of that first essential principle of human actions,
which can alone render them of any value in the sight
of God, faith in Christ. It is not so much what they do,
but what they *neglect* to do, which constitutes, at once,
the danger to themselves and others; it is the *coming
short* which is so full of peril. Alas, how many such are
there, all around, pleasant neighbors, generous friends,
worthy citizens, whose prudence, kindness, integrity, honored and respected by the world, constitute no claim to
acceptance before that tribunal, which searches the heart,
and has declared, "without holiness no man shall see the
Lord."

The habit of employing hair-dressers upon the Sabbath, of giving "card money" to servants, and requiring them to dismiss a visitor with "Not at home," Sunday Concerts and Sunday diversions were each in turn commented upon and condemned in a spirit, at once, so kind, so candid, so decided, that the book commended itself alike to reason and consistency, and challenged a fair and impartial reading even from those most unwilling to abide by its decisions.

On the next meeting with her friend and correspondent, Horace Walpole, he took her to task for having exhibited such monstrously severe doctrines. "He defended, and that was the joke," writes she to her sisters, "religion against me, and said he would do so against the whole bench of bishops—that the fourth commandment was the most amiable and merciful law that was ever promulgated, as it entirely considers the ease and comfort of the hard laboring poor and beasts of burden; but that it was never intended for persons of fashion, who have no occasion for rest as they never do anything on the other days; and indeed when the law was made there were no people of fashion. He really pretended to be in earnest, and we parted mutually unconverted; he lamenting I had fallen into the error of *puritanical* strictness, and I lamenting he

10*

is a person of fashion, for whom the ten commandments
are not made !"

The book made its way ; when the second edition was
issued it sold in little more than a week ; the third in
a few hours ; and seven large editions disappeared in a
few months : extensively read and circulated, it did not
fail to exercise a vast influence in the circles for whom
it was chiefly intended ; its admonitions were heard and
heeded ; several of these customs fell into disrepute, and at
last were entirely abandoned.   For these beneficial changes,
society is indebted to Miss Hannah More.

Two years afterwards an " Estimate of the Religion of
the Fashionable World" appeared, striking deep at the false
principles which govern men in their daily lives, and laying
bare the inconsistencies and hollow professions of those who
bore the christian name.

The estimate is full of sound, clear, and dicriminating
views, applicable quite as much to our time as it was to the
spirit and tendencies of seventy years ago.

"The present age," she says, " may justly be called the
age of benevolence.   Liberality flows with a full tide
through a thousand channels.   There is scarcely a news-
paper that does not record some meeting of men of fortune for the most salutary purposes.   The noble and num-

berless structures for the relief of distress, which are the
ornament and glory of our metropolis, proclaim species of
munificence unknown to former ages. Subscriptions are
easily solicited.

"Allowing the boasted superiority of modern benevolence, it might be well to inquire whether the diffusion of
this branch of charity, though the most lovely offspring of
religion, be yet any positive proof of the prevalence of religious principle? and whether it be not the fashion rather
to consider benevolence as a substitute for Christianity than
as an evidence of it?"

Are not these questions pertinent also to us, in our day?

"It seems to be one of the reigning errors among some,"
she continues, " to reduce all religion into benevolence, and
all benevolence into alms-giving. The wide and comprehensive idea of christian charity is compressed into the
slender compass of a little pecuniary relief. This species
of benevolence is indeed a bright gem among the orna-
ments of a Christian; but by no means furnishes all the
jewels of a crown, which derives its lustre from the associated radiance of every christian grace.

"The mere casual benevolence of any man can have
little claim to solid esteem; nor does any charity deserve
the name, which does not grow out of a steady conviction

that it is his bounden duty; which does not spring from a settled propensity to obey the whole will of God; which is not therefore made a part of the general plan of his conduct; and which does not lead him to order the whole scheme of his affairs with an eye to it.

"He therefore who does not habituate himself to certain interior restraints, who does not live in a regular course of self-renunciation, will not be likely often to perform acts of beneficence, when it becomes necessary to convert to such purposes any of that time or money which appetite, temptation, or vanity solicit him to divert to other purposes.

"And surely he who seldom sacrifices one darling indulgence, who does not subtract one gratification from the incessant round of his enjoyments, when the indulgence would obstruct his capacity of doing good, or when the sacrifice would enlarge his power, does not deserve the name of *benevolent*. And for such an unequivocal criterion of charity, to whom are we to look, but to the conscientious Christian? No other spirit but that by which he is governed, can subdue self-love: and where self-love is the predominant passion, benevolence can have but a feeble, or an accidental dominion.

"Now if we look around, and remark the excesses of luxury, the costly diversions, and the intemperate dissipation in which numbers of professing Christians indulge themselves, can any stretch of candor, can even that tender sentiment by which we are enjoined 'to hope' and to 'believe all things,' enable us to hope and believe that such are actuated by a spirit of christian benevolence, merely because we see them perform some casual acts of charity, which the spirit of the world can contrive to make extremely compatible with a voluptuous life ; and the cost of which, after all, bears but little proportion to that of any one vice, or even vanity !' "

The length of the extract will be pardoned on account of its excellence and appropriateness to our own time. The whole treatise is worthy of a thorough reading, replete as it is with sound sense and healthy piety, although there are allusions here and there, better befitting an English audience than our own. The Bishop of London declared there were few persons in Great Britain who could write such a book, conveying so much sound, evangelical morality, and so much genuine Christianity, in such neat and elegant language, and predicted that the book would find its way into every fine lady's library, and if it did not into her heart and manners, the fault would be her own.

A letter from Mrs. Chapone thus expresses her commendation :—

" The same good gentleman, my dear Madam, who some
time ago gave his excellent thoughts to ' the Great,' has
again made a powerful effort for their reformation, which
they receive with as much avidity as if they meant to be
amended by it : indeed he has wisely recommended
it to their taste by every charm and ornament of
eloquence.

" He has been so obliging as to send me a copy of his
admirable book, and as I do not know his name and address, I take the liberty of applying to you (who are, I believe, pretty well acquainted with him, though probably
not aware of half his merits), to beg you will convey to
him my grateful acknowledgments for his favor, and assure him that he continually rises in my esteem, by the
faithful zeal with which he lays out the talents intrusted to
him at the highest interest ; and I will venture to confess
(gentleman though he be), that I sincerely love and honor
him, and wish the most perfect success to all his laudable
undertakings.

" We long for you in town, my dear Miss More ; hasten
and enjoy the applause your lay friend has gained, and to
which his own heart must bear testimony."

Two choice spirits had been added to her list of friends,
Rev. John Newton and William Wilberforce, both of

whom quickened her energies for the new and honorable career which opened before her.

Of Wilberforce and the great subject that first linked them together, she thus writes to Mrs. Carter :—

"This most important cause, the project to abolish the slave-trade in Africa, has very much occupied my thoughts this summer; the young gentleman, Mr. Wilberforce, who has embarked in it with the zeal of an apostle, has been much with me, and engaged all my little interest, and all my affections in it. It is to be brought before Parliament in the spring. Above one hundred members have promised their votes. My dear friend, be sure to canvass everybody who has a heart. It is a subject too ample for a letter, and I shall have a great deal to say to you on it when we meet. To my feelings it is the most interesting subject which was ever discussed in the annals of humanity."

Similarity of pursuits and sentiments soon drew the two together, and laid the foundations of an intimacy, whose delightful and improving interchanges proved not only a source of strength and comfort to themselves, but a fountain of blessings to others.

At twenty-six Wilberforce was a member of Parliament, master of an ample fortune, surrounded by friends and flat-

terers, treading a path thickly strown with temptations,
pleasures, vices, all tending to corrupt the morals, and
mislead the judgment. On a continental tour to recruit
during a recess of Parliament, in company with a friend,
a little book became also the companion of their journey;
a little book which asked no favors, uttered no flatteries,
and could expect little countenance from one like Wilberforce. "It is one of the best little books ever written
though," spake his friend, who revered its bravery and
truth, though he had no mind to obey its dictates. Wilberforce unwittingly said, "Let us read it then;" and so
the two journeyed and read. "I will search the Scriptures and see if these things are so," resolved Wilberforce,
as he read and was astonished. The book was Doddridge's
Rise and Progress of Religion, whose appeals and persuasions, whose rebukes and denunciations, the young man
found were recorded and reiterated on every page of the
Bible. Wilberforce saw his danger, and fled for refuge to
the cross of Christ.

Immediately on his return to England, he sought the
spiritual guidance of John Newton. Wilberforce soon appeared a changed man, a living epistle of the grace of
God, known and read of all men. In his consecration to
the service of his Divine Master, there was no reserve or

compromise : he gave up himself and his all : " Henceforth let me do with my might while the day lasts," was the sleepless endeavor of his life.

A society for the reformation of public morals was soon on foot through his instrumentality, which helped greatly to check the spread of blasphemous and indecent publications, and was the source whence sprang many kindred schemes for the public good.

But the abolition of the Slave-trade was the great work which must immortalize Wilberforce, and at twenty-eight, 1787, he began to devote himself to its interests. While making a short sojourn at Bath, for the benefit of its waters during the autumn of this year, he records of himself, " I believe one cause of my having fallen so short is my having aimed no higher. Remember, thy situation abounding in comforts requires thee to be peculiarly on thy guard, lest when thou hast eaten and art full, thou forgettest God"—yet Miss More who passed much time in his society at this time declares, " This young gentleman's character is one of the most extraordinary I ever knew for talents, virtue, and piety. It is difficult not to grow wiser and better every time one converses with him."

The enormities of the Slave Traffic had for a long time attracted the attention of thoughtful and feeling minds

both in England and America. Seven years before, **Mr.**
Burke had almost determined to bring the subject before
the English Parliament, having sketched a bill to provide
for the immediate amelioration of its severities and its
ultimate extinction ;—the plan however he abandoned,
from a conviction that it would prove an unpopular and
ruinous measure for his party.

Meanwhile facts were collected and arguments adduced
to arouse and inform the public mind ; in May 1787,
several gentlemen met together in London and formed
themselves into a committee to collect information and
raise funds for promoting the abolition of the trade ; over
this body, Granville Sharpe presided, while Clarkson, as
their agent, was in the field with all his quenchless ardor,
bringing out from their dark dens, facts and truths, respecting the traffic, which curdled the blood and almost
awakened the distrust of every English reader, yet it had
struck its roots into the commercial interests of the country,
and hundreds were ready to defend it.

And now the subject must be laid before Parliament—
where is the man of moral mettle, to undertake it ? No
man of party connection or political ambition dared engage in a work of such doubtful and dangerous issues.
It must be undertaken at his own peril, depending alone

on the righteousness of his cause, for commercial power and self-interest, wealth and long usage were all against it A man must do it from God's imposition and for humanity's sake. Wilberforce was the man. How bravely he battled, and how glorious the issue, the world knows well.

Among the publications of the day to arouse and enlist the public sympathies, "The Slave Trade," a little poem, issued from the pen of Hannah More.

The muse in impassioned strains thus exclaims :—

> "What wrongs, what injuries does Oppression plead,
> To smooth the crime and sanctify the deed?
> What strange offence, what aggravated sin?
> They stand convicted—of a darker skin!
> Barbarians, hold! the opprobrious commerce spare,
> Respect *His* sacred image which they bear.
> Though dark and savage, ignorant and blind,
> They claim the common privilege of kind;
> Let malice strip them of each other plea,
> They still are men, and men should still be free.
> Insulted Reason loathes th' inverted trade—
> Loathes, as she views the human purchase made;
> The outraged goddess, with abhorrent eyes,
> Sees *man* the traffic, *souls* the merchandise!

CHAPTER IX.

Labors among the Poor—Sunday Schools.

On New Year's day of 1789, Miss More is dining at Berkley-square, Mrs. Montagu having assembled around her a few of the Bleus, among whom we recognize the familiar face of Mrs. Boscawen.

Mrs. Vesey, who made one of this brilliant circle on Hannah's first introduction to London, was now in that state of suffering, which left one nothing to hope—her mind was gone.

"Ah," sighed Miss More, on visiting her, "it is melancholy to look at this house where I have seen so many agreeable people, and heard so much pleasant conversation, and made so many friendships, and think that its mistress is bereft of her faculties. What a call for serious reflection! I want to get my heart more affected with feeling for the sorrows of others, and with gratitude for my own mercies."

She soon after went down to Hampton where she had

as yet endeavored to pass a few weeks, each year, to cheer the widowed heart of Mrs. Garrick. The exciting topic of the spring was the slave question, which was about to be laid before Parliament. Wilberforce went down to Teston, at Sir Charles Middleton's country seat, to consult his advisers and marshal his forces for the approaching debate. " He with the whole junto of abolitionists are slaving it till two o'clock every morning," declares Mrs. Bouverie. " I hope Teston will be the Runnymede of the negroes," ejaculates Miss More, " and the great charter of African liberty will be completed—the fate of Africa now trembles in the balance."

On the 12th of May, in a speech of three hours of surpassing eloquence, Wilberforce opened the debate in the House of Commons, denouncing the slave-trade as a national iniquity and tracing with masterly power its destructive effects upon Africa, upon its victims and upon the colonies ; viewed from his own stand point, not political advancement or party tactics, but from the elevated height of a common humanity and christian civilization, he beheld its horrors and injustice in all their length and breadth and depth, and his own soul glowed with the magnitude of the subject. Pitt, Burke, and Fox, gave him a strong and eloquent support, each unanimously declaring that the slave-trade was the disgrace and opprobrium of the country, and that nothing but its entire abolition could satisfy the demands of justice and the appeals of humanity. It was deemed a glorious night for England. Principles familiar to us as household words were then broached as dangerous and startling innovations, and were met by a powerful opposition from the callous, the timid, and the self-interested.

Miss More soon left these exciting scenes for a June flitting at Rosedale, Mrs. Boscawen's new villa at Richmond, "And I am sitting," she closes a letter to Martha, "on the very seat where Thomson wrote his Seasons." The abode of the poet was a simple cottage in Kew-foot Lane on the banks of the Thames. It was purchased at his death by George Ross, Esq., who enlarged and beautified it, reverently preserving whatever he consistently could of the old domain. At his death, the property fell to Mrs. Boscawen. There was the Bard's favorite seat in the alcove under the old elm-tree, and there a little walnut table, where Thomson sang the seasons and their change: and may we not suppose that fancy lent enchantment to the scene, as the friends lingered in the alcove, heard the warblings of the thrush, and gazed upon the summer beauties of the landscape, which inspired the heart of the poet?

The remainder of the season was diversified by a visit to Sandleford, whose Gothic windows, Grecian wit and British oaks, could not ward off five days of unrelenting headache, to which Miss More from early life was subject; then a sail down the river Wye, in company with her pleasant and excellent friends Mr. and Miss Wilberforce, looking at abbeys and castles, enjoying at once the benefits of improving conversation and the charms of most beautiful and interesting scenery; we find her next at Stoke, dwelling in sober magnificence with a certain Dowager Duchess, where a little more discretion and a little less fancy were proper and decorous, as she tells us.

Hannah and Martha are now at Cowslip Green: the retreat is enlivened by a day from Mrs. Montagu, a week from Mrs. Garrick, both of whom came to try the benefit of Bath waters, and a fortnight from Mrs. Kennicott, "who with wonderful readiness accommodated herself to the quiet, simple life of their little cottage;" then came a vacation week from the elder sisterhood, and last, though not least, the Wilberforces made a ramble to the Green.

Among the interesting features of the surrounding scenery, rose the bold and romantic Cliffs of Cheddar, forming a picturesque perspective towards the south ten

miles from Cowslip Green. Among these cliffs were scenes
of wild beauty and solemn grandeur, yawning caverns,
damp hollows and bald peaks, which made them the
summer resort of many a traveller in quest of sublime and
imposing scenery.

The sisters begged Wilberforce not to leave Wrington
without a visit to these wonders of the region. Patty was
eloquent, and urged the gratification which the drive would
afford to a mind like his : a day was fixed—then given
up ; the Cliffs were again discussed at the breakfast-table,
the next morning, until their guest was prevailed upon
to go.

On his return, Patty ran into the parlor, triumphantly
inquiring, " How he liked the Cliffs ?"

" Very fine," he replied ; " but the poverty and distress
of the people are dreadful."

"This was all that passed," said Patty, in relating the
circumstance. " Wilberforce soon retired to his room, and
dismissed even his reader. I said to Hannah and his sister that I feared he was not well. The cold chicken and
wine put into the carriage for his dinner, was returned un-
touched. Mr. Wilberforce appeared at supper, seemingly
refreshed with a higher feast than we had sent with him.
The servant, at his desire, was dismissed, when immediately

he began : ' Miss Hannah More, something must be done for Cheddar.'

" He then gave us a particular account of his day, of the inquiries he had made respecting the poor: there was no resident minister, no manufactory, nor did there appear any dawn of comfort, either temporal or spiritual. The possibility and method of assisting them was discussed till a late hour: it was then decided in a few words, by Mr. Wilberforce's exclaiming, ' If you will be at the trouble, I will be at the expense.'

" Something commonly called an impulse, crossed my heart, that told me it was God's work, and it would do : and though I never have, and probably never shall recover the same emotion, yet it is my business to water it with watchfulness.

" Mr. Wilberforce and his sister left us in a day or two. We turned many schemes in our head every possible way ; at length those measures were adopted, which led to the formation of the different schools."

The Cliffs of Cheddar, at this time, were inhabited by a squalid, ignorant, half-savage people, dwelling in the caves and fissures of the rocks, and earning a miserable subsistence by selling roots, stalactites, and other mineral productions of the place, to travellers who came hither,

and recounting also the legends with which the region
abounds.

The hearts of the sisters, we may suppose, had already
yearned over the destitution and wretchedness of this forlorn race, thus hanging as it were on the skirts of civilization : for they readily and joyfully responded to the call.
Home missionary work of this kind was then comparatively
new ; though Robert Raikes had begun to bless Gloucester
with the Sunday-school, and two hundred and fifty thousand children were already enjoying its privileges, yet the
inestimable benefits of the institution were not yet widely
extended or fully realized ; old Brentford also was reaping
a harvest of good from the warm-hearted efforts of good
Mrs. Trimmer, who had established, and was superintending a system of moral instruction, whereby large numbers
of poor children had been reclaimed from idleness and vice.
These efforts had received Hannah More's cordial sympathy and warm approval : a similar field was now spread
out before her ; a sphere of active usefulness, unlike any
which she had hitherto occupied, invited her attention, and
appealed to her christian love. She resolved upon immediate action. Accompanied by Patty, she is soon explor-
ing the region, a graphic account of which she gives in a

letter to Wilberforce, while still on the tour, dated from George Hotel, Cheddar.

"Though this is but a romantic place, as my friend Matthew well observed, yet you would laugh to see the bustle I am in. I was told that we should meet with great opposition if I did not try to propitiate the chief despot of the village, who is very rich and very brutal : so I ventured into the den of this monster, in a country as savage as himself, near Bridgewater. He begged that I would not think of bringing any religion into the country : it was the worst thing in the world for the poor, it made them lazy and useless. In vain I represented to him, that they would be more industrious as they were better principled ; and that, for my own part, I had no selfish views in what I was doing. He gave me to understand that he knew the world too well to believe either the one or the other. Somewhat dismayed to find that my success bore no proportion to my submissions, I was almost discouraged from more visits ; but I found that friends must be secured at all events ; for if these rich savages set their faces against us, and influenced the poor people, I saw that nothing but hostilities would ensue ; so I made eleven more of these agreeable visits ; and, as I improved in the art of canvassing, had better success. Miss Wilberforce would have been shocked, had she seen the petty tyrants whose insolence I stroked and tamed, the ugly children I praised, the pointers and spaniels I caressed, the cider I commended, and the wine I swallowed. After these irresistible flatteries, I inquired of each if he could recommend me to a house ; and said that I had a little plan which I hoped would secure their orchards from being robbed, their rabbits from being shot, their game from being stolen, and which might lower the poor-rates. If effect be the best proof of eloquence, then mine was a good speech, for I gained, at length, the hearty concurrence of the whole people, and their promise to discourage and favor the poor in proportion as they were attentive or negligent in sending their children. Patty, who is with me, says she has good hopes that the hearts of some of these rich poor wretches may be touched : they are as ignorant as the beasts that perish, intoxicated every day before dinner, and plunged into such vices as make me begin to think London a virtuous place. By their assistance I procured immediately a good house, which, when a partition is taken down, and a window added, will receive a great number of children. The house and an excellent garden of almost an acre of ground, I have taken at once for six guineas and a half a year   I have ventured to take it for seven years—there is courage for you! It is to be put in order immediately, 'for the night cometh;' and it is a comfort to think that though I may be in dust and ashes in a few weeks, yet by that time this business will be in actual motion. I have written to different manufacturing towns for a mistress, but can get nothing hitherto. As to the mistress for the Sunday-school and the religious part, I have employed Mrs. Esterbrook, of whose judgment I have a good opinion. I hope Miss W—— will not be frightened,—but I am afraid she must be called a Methodist.

"I asked the farmers if they had no resident curate? They told me they had a right to insist on one; which right they confessed, they had never ventured to exercise, for fear their tithes would be raised. I blushed for my species. The glebe-house is good for my purposes. The curate lives at Wells, twelve miles distant. They have only service once a week, and there is scarcely an instance of a poor person being visited or prayed with."

In spite of Miss Hannah's repeated headaches, and Miss Patty's ill-health, so promptly and energetically did they pursue their labors, that the 1st of October witnessed the opening of the school in Cheddar, by Miss Hannah in person. The principal people from the parishes far and

12

near, came to witness the operation of a scheme, as it was regarded, to reform Botany Bay.

"It was an affecting sight," says she. "Several of the grown-up youth had been tried at the late assizes,—three were the children of a person lately condemned to be hanged ; many thieves, all ignorant, profane and vicious, beyond belief. Of this banditti we have enlisted one hundred and seventy ; and when the clergyman, a hard man, who is also the magistrate, saw these creatures kneeling around us, whom he had seen but to commit or to punish in some way, he burst into tears. I can do them but little good, I fear, but the grace of God can.

"Have you never felt your mind," she asks Wilberforce, "now and then raised and touched by some very trifling circumstance? So I felt on Sunday. Some musical gentleman, drawn from a distance by curiosity (just as I was coming out of church with my ragged regiment, much depressed to think how little good I could do them), quite unexpectedly struck up that beautiful and animated anthem, 'In as much as you do it to one of the least of these, you have done it unto me.'"

To the Sunday-school was soon added a school during the week, where sewing, knitting, and spinning were taught to the girls. A faithful and excellent woman was engaged as mistress of this school, who, with her daughter, entered so completely into Miss More's plans, that medicine, clothing, and small sums of money were, from time to time, placed at her disposal, to distribute among the sick and needy, to whom she ever proved a friend and comforter.

Two years after Miss More's first visit to Cheddar, she received a zealous ally in the Rev. Thomas Drewitt, who became a resident curate among this people, strengthening her hands, and encouraging her heart by all the means in his power.

Great as was the work for Cheddar, Cheddar did not bound their hopes or exhaust their energies: other fields opened before them, and they went boldly forward bearing the precious seed; thirteen parishes were found equally destitute of the means of social comforts or religious improvement. In Shipham the women knew nothing of industry or frugality, the young men spent the Sabbath in sporting and hunting, and the children in nakedness and vagrancy. At Axbridge the curate was intoxicated six times in the week, and very frequently was prevented from preaching by two black eyes, honestly earned by fighting; the ale-house was more frequented than the church, the laws of cards or quoits were better understood than the ten commanaments, while good order and domestic peace were things unheard of.

"The lower classes are *fated* to be poor, ignorant, and wicked," said the petty landholders; "and wise as you are, you cannot alter what is decreed." "Besides," added another, "I like the parish very well as it is,—if the young men come and gamble before my house Sunday afternoon, I have only to go out and curse and swear at them, and they will march off,—what can one desire more?"

Happily for the parishes, there were those who *did* desire more—happily there were eyes that wept, and hearts that felt, and lips that prayed, for the sorrows and woes of the poor: there were time, and talent, and money that had been consecrated to the Lord's service, and they were to be employed among his poor: before the year closed schools were established in nine different parishes,—and five hundred scholars were enjoying the benefits of Sabbath-school instruction.

From Bath, Wilberforce wrote to Miss More:—"I have more money than time, and if you or your sister will condescend to be my almoner, you will enable me to employ some of the superfluity it has pleased God to give me, to some good purpose. Sure am I, that they who subscribe attention and industry furnish articles of more sterling and intrinsic value. Besides, I have a rich banker in London, Mr. Henry Thornton, whom I cannot oblige so much as by drawing on him for purposes like these. I shall take the liberty of enclosing a draft for £40 ; but this is only for a beginning."

" I joyfully accept your office of almoner," responds Hannah, thankful to scatter around the " gleanings of the horn of plenty," " on condition that you will find fault with, and direct me with as little scruple as I shall have in disposing of your money. Patty is very proud at being admitted into the confederacy, and at being appointed superintendent of Cheddar ; a title, however, she will only hold by delegation in my too long absence, for I like my dignity too well to allow her to be more than vice-queen.

" What comfort I feel, in looking round on these starving and half-naked multitudes, to think that by your liberality many of them may be fed and clothed : and oh, if but one soul is rescued from eternal misery, how may we rejoice over it in another state, where perhaps it may not be one of our smallest felicities that our friendship was turned to some useful account in advancing the good of others, and, as I humbly presume to hope, in improving ourselves for that life which shall have no end.

" Mr. Henry Thornton, I think, belongs to the Society

12*

of Sunday-schools in London, for assisting necessitous villages with books, &c. There cannot be a fairer claim on
them than the present. If you and he approve it, perhaps
we may apply for a quantity of New Testaments, prayer-
books, and little Sunday-school books, with a few Bibles.
The sooner we get them the better ; otherwise, you or he
will be so good as to order a supply from the Society for
promoting Christian Knowledge, to which I do not belong,
or I would send for them. They may be directed to Park-
street."

To Mrs. Carter she writes, " It is grievous to reflect, that
while we are sending missionaries to India, our villages are
in pagan darkness, and upon many of them scarcely a ray
of Christianity has shone. I speak from the most minute
and diligent examination. I have been constantly occupied for a long time, in trying what my poor abilities and
my small influence over others, richer and better, can bring
about. In one particular spot, for instance, there are six
large parishes, without so much as a resident curate.
Through the kind assistance of a friend or two, I am endeavoring to fix schools and other little institutions in the
most destitute of these places, and, as they are from six to
ten miles distant, you will judge that it employs a good
deal of my time. I have the satisfaction to tell you, that

Cheddar, our first establishment, goes on prosperously. We have a great many children in that parish only, and by the ability and piety of our teachers, their improvement surpasses my warmest hopes. I make no apology to you, my dear friend, for the freedom of these details. Alas! there are so few to whom one *can* speak or write upon such subjects.

"Poor Patty is a great sufferer. Our friend, Mrs. Garrick, who is still at Bristol Wells, has been to see us several times: she does not think herself quite recovered. To those who have enjoyed during a lifetime perfect health, illness is particularly alarming. Let you and me, my dear friend, number our infirm health, among the merciful providences which have been dispensed to us. How much more do we enjoy our intervals of ease than those who know no pains, and I hope we may be able to turn the pain itself to a good account. 'All things work together for good to them that love God.'

"I wish you could see my roses. I have a double end in such a wish, for then I should see *you*. I am truly and faithfully, my dearest Mrs. Carter, yours."——

At this time the elder sisters retired from their school, after a professional experience of nearly thirty years, highly creditable to themselves, and amply rewarded by an ex-

tensive patronage, which enabled them to build a fine
house in Bath, and spend their later years in the enjoyment of every comfort which earth can give, besides that
unspeakable peace which heaven bestows upon its heirs.

Henceforth the sisters had two homes, sometimes at
Cowslip Green, sometimes at Bath ; and the fraternal tie
was strengthened and hallowed by the hearty co-operation
of each other in holy purposes and useful plans.

The Mendip schools were dear to the sisterhood : each
bore her share in their labors, fatigues, anxieties, and conflicts, sustaining and encouraging their sister Hannah, in
the conspicuous and important part which her talents and
energy required her to bear. How delightful this circle,
undivided by the change of years, and unbroken by death,
mingling together their fortunes and affections in the same
great pursuits, and around the same home-hearths.

In the establishment of their schools, the difficulties to
be overcome needed all the resolution and judgment of
minds like theirs. Though the field of effort was in a land
of Bibles and Sabbaths, yet a preparatory work, not wholly
unlike that which is necessary on heathen ground, was
needed here,—the whole people whom they wished to
benefit, were to be *conciliated*,—fearing not God, or regard-
ing man, they neither desired nor cared for the blessings

which christian love would bestow,—there were the prejudices and opposition of the small proprietors, the hardness
and guilt of the poor, the hatred of the ale-houses, the indifference of the church,—the general ignorance and inca-
pability of appreciating the nature of the good to be conferred upon them, the difficulty also of obtaining suitable
teachers, prudent, discreet, and pious ; add to these
said Miss Hannah, after the good work was in progress,
" The teaching of the teachers, which is not the least part
of the work—having about thirty masters and mistresses,
with under-teachers, one has continually to bear with the
faults, the ignorance, the prejudices, humors, misfortunes,
and *debts* of all these poor, well-meaning people. I hope,
however, it teaches one forbearance, and it serves to put
me in mind how much God has to bear from me. I now
and then comfort Patty in our journeys home at night, by
saying, if we do these people no good, I hope we do some
little good to ourselves."

But Miss More neither flinched nor faltered in her arduous service : she who had not hesitated to speak plain,
but unwelcome truths to the gay and great, and reiterate
the startling admonitions of the Bible in the halls of
luxurious ease, would shrink from no personal fatigue
or be disheartened either by opposition or indifference.

The course of instruction pursued in her schools was divided into four classes, Bible, Testament, Psalter, and the Catechism and Alphabet; the rules were always read at their opening on Sunday morning, followed by a prayer, a hymn, and a part of the 34th Psalm.

"For the first year," said Miss More, in speaking of the mother and daughter whom she had engaged as teachers for Cheddar, and the difficulties presented at Cheddar were like those of every other place, where schools had been planted, "these excellent women had to struggle with every kind of opposition, so that they were frequently tempted to give up their laborious employ. They well entitled themselves to £30 per annum salary and some little presents. They visited the sick, chiefly with a view to their spiritual concerns; but we concealed the true motive at first: and in order to procure them access to the homes and hearts of the people, they were furnished not only with medicine, but with a little money, which they administered with great prudence. They soon gained their confidence, read and prayed to them, and in all respects did what a good clergyman does in other parishes.

"At the end of the year we perceived that much ground had been gained among the poor; but the success was attended with no small persecution from the rich, though some of them grew more favorable.

"I now ventured to have a sermon read after school on a Sunday evening, inviting a few of the parents, and keeping the grown-up children; the sermons were of the most awakening sort, and soon produced sensible effects. It was at first thought a very methodistical measure, and we got a few broken windows; but quiet perseverance, and the great prudence with which the zeal of our good mistresses was regulated, carried us through. Many reprobates were, by the blessing of God, awakened, and many swearers and Sabbath-breakers reclaimed. The number both of young and old scholars increased, and the daily life and conversation of many seemed to keep pace with their religious professions on the Sunday.

"We now began to distribute Bibles, prayer-books, and other good books, but never at random, and only to those who had given some evidence of their loving and deserving them. They are always made the reward of superior learning, or some other merit, as we can have no other proof that they will be read. Those who manifest the greatest diligence, get the books of most importance. During my absence in the winter, a great many will learn twenty or thirty chapters, psalms and hymns.

" Finding the wants and distresses of these poor people uncommonly great (for their wages are but one shilling per day), and fearing to abuse the bounty of my friends by too indiscriminate liberality, it occurred to me that I could make what I had to bestow go much further, by instituting clubs or societies for the women, as is done for the men in other places. It was no small trouble to accomplish this ; for though the subscription was only three half-pence a week, it was more than they could always raise; yet the object appeared so important, that I found it would be good economy privately to give widows and other very poor women money to pay their club. After combating many prejudices, we carried this point, which we took care to involve in the general system, by making it subservient to the schools, the rules of the club restraining the women to such and such points of conduct respecting the schools. In some parishes we have one hundred and fifty poor women thus associated ; you may guess who are the patronesses."

These clubs proved a great blessing to the little communities, in which they were established, by helping the poor to husband their small resources for a time of need, and teaching them the importance and advantage of economy: in sickness, a member received three shillings a week, for lying-in seven shillings and sixpence.

A girl trained in their schools and sustaining a virtuous character, was presented on her marriage day with five shillings, a pair of white stockings, and a new Bible.

"Henceforth," says Miss More, "I desire to have little to do with the great. I have devoted the remnant of my life to the poor, and those that have no helper; and if I can do them no good, I can at least sympathize with them, and I know it is some comfort for a forlorn creature, to be able to say, 'there is something that cares for me.' The simple idea of *being cared for*, has always appeared to me a very cheering one: besides, the affection they have for me is a strong engine with which to lift them to a love of higher things. Alas, I might do more and better—pray for me."

When at Wrington, which now began to be the greater part of the year, accompanied by one of her sisters, usually Patty, she endeavored to visit at least three parishes every Sabbath, riding from ten to thirty miles, often enduring thirteen hours, exposure to the weather, and frequently passing the night at some of the villages, and all this for upwards of twenty years:—what heroic devotion, what inflexibility of purpose, what earnest love does it not

13

reveal! At an age too, when most women are willing to
retire from arduous labor in their Master's service, and
eagerly beg to be excused even from the far less burdensome duty of Sabbath-school instruction of our own time.

Her voluntary withdrawal from circles, whose wit, learning, and elegance must present strong fascinations to a
mind gifted like hers, and where she had had every induce-
ment to remain, evinces the strength and sincerity of her
religious convictions; while her blessed charities and abundant labors among the despised and forsaken, for whose
souls no man careth, shows the tender benevolence and
unselfish sympathies of an humble and believing heart.

How beautiful among the cottages are the feet of her,
who bringeth glad tidings!

Christian disciple, regardest thou not too lightly the
good that thou mightest do among the waste places
and hedges of life. If thou art Christ's, thou must be
Christ-like; as He yearns over poor lost souls, so must
thou: as He begat a work to save them, so must thy love
not be a powerless and inefficient love, but a working,
saving, personal love; as at the Well, the Pool, the Corn-
field and the Garden, so like thy Divine Master, must thou
work while the day lasts: as He went among the poor,
the despised, and the lowly esteemed among men, so must

not *thou* neglect them : among such thou shalt gain a ready hearing, and of such is the kingdom of heaven. Oh, there are many watchings, toilsome labors, oppressions, heart-breakings, sinful murmurings, long, sorrowful days, yearnings for the bread of life in these humble homes : visit them : tell of the Balm in Gilead, talk of a Saviour's love, narrate the story of the Cross : hearts, sinful and hard, will melt that one careth for their welfare. Thus shall the seed of Divine truth be sown in many a home ; you may never know when or how it shall spring up ; you may never know the travail of soul necessary for its germination, but souls will be born into the kingdom of Heaven ; light will arise in darkness ; believing hearts will be glimmering here and there with faith and love, where your feet have trod ; your Master will be honored, and at the great day spirits redeemed through your labors of love, shall make up the crown of your rejoicing.

CHAPTER X.

Newton in Sorrow—Mendip Feast.

MR. NEWTON is smitten : pierced and wounded with the arrows of affliction, he turns to Hannah More for the tender consolations of her christian sympathy : his wife, the idol of his early days, the beloved companion of his later years, is no more. To him it is an hour of sorrow and of joy : sorrow that she is not, joy for the balm in Gilead, so he writes :—how beautifully is the tenderness of earthly affection chastened and subdued by heavenly love, how royally does the weeping mourner take refuge in Him, who chastens not willingly.

"I could begin every letter," ran his, "with the words of David, 'Oh magnify the Lord with me, and let us exalt his name together.' Great has been his goodness ! I am a wonder to many, and to myself. You perhaps know, madam, from what you have read of mine, and possibly from what you have seen in me, that my attachment to my dearest was great, yea excessive, yea idolatrous ! It was so when it began. I think no writer of romance ever imagined more than I realized. It was so when I married. She was to me precisely (how can I write it?) in the place of God. In all places and companies my thoughts were full of her. I did everything for her sake, and if she was absent (for I made three long voyages to, Africa afterwards), I could take pleasure in nothing. So narrow were my notions of happiness at this time, that I had no idea that I was capable of anything greater or better than of being always with her. By degrees, He who has the only right to my heart, and who alone can fill it, was pleased to make me sensible of his just claim; and my idol was brought some steps lower down, yet still, I fear, there was somewhat of the golden calf in my love, from the moment that joined our hands, to the moment of separation. She was certainly my chief temporal blessing, and the providential hinge upon which all the principal events of my life have turned. Before I was four years old, she was sent into the world to be my companion, and to soften the rugged path of life. The difficulties in the way of our union were so many, so great, so apparently insuperable that my hope of obtaining her seemed little less chimerical than if I had expected the crown of Poland. Yet, at the proper time it took place. Fond as I was of her, I knew that incon-

13*

stancy and mutability are primary attributes of the *human heart depraved*, if left to itself ; but, as the providence of God joined our hands, a secret blessing from him cemented our hearts, we certainly understood Thomson when he says,

> ' Enamored more as more remembrance swells
> With many a proof of recollected love.'

Further, though I had deserved to forfeit her every day of my life, yet he spared her to me more than forty years ; and, lastly (which is the crowning mercy), when he recalled the loan,—for, strictly speaking, she was not mine, but his, —he made me willing to resign her. Through the long course of her very trying illness, he supported me. Though my feelings were often painful, I believe a stranger who had seen me in company, or heard me from the pulpit, would hardly have suspected what was passing at home. On the evening of the 15th instant I watched her, with a candle in my hand, for some hours ; and when I was sure she had breathed her last,—which could not at once be determined, she went away so easily,—I kneeled down by her bedside, with those who were in the room, and thanked the Lord, I trust, with all my heart, for her dismission. I slept this night as well as usual ; and, in defiance of the laws of tyrant custom, I continued to preach while she lay dead in the house. We deposited her in our own vault the 23d, and last Sunday evening I was enabled to preach her funeral-sermon, from Habakkuk, iii. 17, 18.

"In writing to you I feel my heart open : I am assured of meeting from you with that sympathy and sensibility of which I hope I am not myself wholly destitute; and therefore I will tattle on. This was not a sudden stroke. She did not die by a flash of lightning, by what is called accident, nor by those rapid disorders which break the thread of life in a few days or hours. The Lord gave me time to prepare for it; yea, by the gradual train of his dispensations, he gradually prepared me for it himself.

"She was confined to the house nearly ten years, excepting that in September, 1789, she was enabled to go for a month to Southampton, and during the last autumn went out every evening in a coach, for a little air. But she was shut up from the house of God, and from visiting her friends, though, till about September, she could generally receive them at home. Indeed, till about that time, I did not give up all hope of her recovery. But a total loss of appetite, or rather, a loathing of food, then took place, which soon reduced her to a state of great weakness. In the beginning of October she took to her bed, and was soon after, I suppose from some defect in the spine, deprived of all locomotive power. She could neither move herself, nor without the greatest difficulty, be moved; sometimes not so much as to have anything about her changed for a fortnight together. Such, my dear madam, was the state of my idol; what a rebuke—what a lesson was it to me, to see her lie for eight or nine weeks in so sad and pitiable a situation! But the case was mingled with many merciful alleviations. Her patience was wonderful,—her natural spirit as good as when she was in health. Often when my eyes were full of tears, she has constrained me to smile. When she could not move her body, she was thankful that she could move her hands, thankful that the Lord had laid no more upon her than she could bear; and when I once said, 'You are a great sufferer,' she replied, 'I do suffer, but not greatly.' So to know that we are sinners, and so to know the Saviour, as to feel both the necessity and the liberty of applying to him, constitutes that knowledge which chiefly deserves the name; and this, I trust, was her privilege long before her last illness. But the enemy of our peace found advantage from the weakness of her frame, to distress her with doubts which did not so directly apply to her own state as to the

whole system of truth.   She said, 'If there be a Saviour,'
—'If there be a God.'   In this interval, which lasted near
a fortnight, there was some abatement of that serenity I
spoke of, some signs of impatience, and she discovered a
strong reluctance to the thought of dying.   Then was my
sharpest trial; but the cloud gradually wore off, and for
the last month she spoke of her departure with great com-
posure, and seemed perfectly reconciled to it.   Yet, she
never recovered strength and freedom to speak much
to me about herself.   The Sunday before she died, I said,
'If you cannot easily speak, and if your mind be at
peace, I wish you to signify it by holding up your hand.'
She immediately held it up, and waved it for a little time.
This from her, who knew the Gospel so well, comforted
and satisfied me.   It reminded me of the striking scene in
Shakspeare, of Cardinal Beaufort, which closes with, 'He
dies—but gives no sign.'   Blessed be God, it was not her
case !

"In the course of the day she asked for me, though I
was seldom long or far from her; but her head was so
much affected by lying many weeks in one position, that
though perfectly sensible, she could hardly bear the sound
of the gentlest voice, or the softest footsteps upon the carpet.   I went to her; she stroked my face, squeezed my

hand, and said, 'My pretty dear!' an appellation she frequently gave me. We both dropped a few tears. These were the last words I heard her speak, and I could say but little. Such was our last farewell. From that night till she obtained her release, she gave little sign of life but by breathing.

"Now, my dear madam, I have done. I shall trouble you with no more in this strain. She is gone—and may I not add, I am going? For though my health was never better than at present, I am advancing in my 66th year. What is the world to me now? All the treasures of the Bank of England could not repair my loss, or even abate my sense of it. My chief earthly tie to this life is broken; yet, I thank God, I am willing to live, while he has any service for me to do, or rather, while he pleases, whether I can serve him or not, provided I am favored with submission to his will. I have lost my right hand. He has made me willing to part with it, but I must expect to miss it often. However, I thank him, I am by no means uncomfortable. I am satisfied he does all things well; and though some months ago, had it been lawful, I would have redeemed her life and health by the sacrifice of a limb, and thought the purchase cheap; yet, now his will is made known by the event, I trust I can from the heart say, with Fenelon, 'I would not take up a straw to have things otherwise than they are.' Time is short. A new and inconceivable scene will soon open upon us, and if they who now 'sow in tears shall reap in joy,' they may smile while they weep.

"We seem to want some other word by which to denote our supreme regard for God, than that which expresses our affection to creatures. When we speak of loving him, it must be in a different sense. Creature-love is a passion ; Divine love is a principle. It arises from an apprehension of his adorable perfections, especially as they are displayed in the great work of redemption, without which it is impossible for a sinner to love him.

"There is a sensibility of feeling in creature-love, which is no proper standard of our love to God. This depending much upon condition and the state of the animal spirits, is different in different persons, and in the same persons at different times. It is variable as the weather, and indeed is often affected by the weather and a thousand local circumstances, no more in our power than the clouds that fly over our heads. It is no uncommon thing to judge more favorably of ourselves on this point on a bright summer's day, and while contemplating a beautiful prospect, than in the gloom of winter, or the hurry of Cheap-

side. The high affection of some people may be compared
to a summer's brook after a hasty rain, which is full and
noisy for a little time, but soon becomes dry. But true
divine love is like a river which always runs, though not
always with equal depth and flow, and never ceases till it
finds the ocean. The best evidences are—admiration of his
way of saving sinners,—humble dependence on his care,—
desire of communion with him in his instituted means of
grace,—submission to the will of his providence, and
obedience to the dictation of his precepts. To keep his
commandments, and to keep them as *His* commandments
from a sense of his authority and goodness, is the best,
the most unsuspicious test of our love to Him."

Who can read this letter, without feeling the power and
value of genuine piety? It is among the most beautiful
records of what God can do for the soul trusting in Him;
how his grace can subdue and control the strongest earthly
passion, and grant consolation, yea joy, in the hours of
deepest sorrow.

A year after, Newton comes to Cowslip Green.

"Pray, my dear sir," wrote Miss More in a note, which
met him on the way, "try to divert your mind from the
delights and elegances of Teston, before you turn your
way towards my little thatched cottage, where a quiet

cell, a few books, a maple dish and a ' dinner of herbs' are all you can in reason expect—but then, I hope we shall be able to furnish the appropriate sauce of ' quietness therewith,' for which I trust you will be contented to renounce the stalled ox of noisy London."

He passed a week there in August ; a week of delightful christian intercourse, the memory of which, ever afterwards, cheered him on his solitary pilgrimage : how they rode to Shipham and visited the schools, how the thunder storm frightened Miss Catlett, how Mr. Newton smoked his pipe, and Patty talked of Cowper,—ah yes, how pleasant is the memory of daily incidents in the visit of a friend.

In passing King Weston's hill on his homeward journey, nothing in the wide and beautiful prospect delighted his eye like a glimpse of the Mendip Ridge, " yes, yes, and I was so foolish as almost to envy a hill, which, if it had eyes like me, might look at Cowslip Green from morning till night."

Nor is the interest dimmed by the dirt of Cheapside, or duties of Colman-street ;

> " In Helicon could I my pen dip
> I might attempt the praise of Mendip ;

14

Were bards an hundred, I'd outstrip 'em
If equal to the fame of Shipham;
But harder still the task, I ween,
To give its due to Cowslip Green,"

writes he in quaint and curious numbers.

"Every Sunday morning my thoughts set out in quest of you and Miss Patty, and though I know not what road you have taken, I seldom miss finding you. There is a communion of spirit among the believing members of that body of which Christ is the living head, which I believe is not impeded by local distance."

"I assure you," replied Miss More, "your kind wishes, and your affectionate remembrance of the mountains of Mendip and of the little hermitage at the foot of it, are returned with great sincerity. Your pipe still maintains its station in the black-currant bush, and that hand would be deemed very presumptuous and disrespectful which should presume to displace it. For my own part, the pipe of Tityrus, though in my youthful days I liked it passing well, would not now be deemed a more venerable relic; and even the little sick maid Lizzy, who gratefully remembers the spiritual comfort you administered to her, often cries out, 'Oh dear! I hope nobody will break Mr. Newton's pipe.'

" Patty and I remember you as we are trotting over the hills. She desires her affectionate regards, as do all the rest. You would enjoy the vale of Cowslips in this renewed spring : we have everything of the golden age except the innocence ; the garden is full of roses as in June, and an apple-tree literally covered at the same moment with fruit nearly ripe and fresh blossoms."

Patty had long desired to enrich her album from the pen of Cowper, whose poems were in high favor at Cowslip Green. Newton, the poet's friend and former pastor at Olney, undertook to lay her request before him, who, to show his readiness in obliging an old friend and a fair lady, sent the following couplet, which held a conspicuous place on her pages.

> " In vain to live from age to age
>   We modern bards endeavor ;
>   In Patty's book I wrote one page,
>   And gained my point forever."

In order to increase a general interest in the schools, and reward the punctual attendance of the scholars, the ladies busied themselves in preparing a Feast, or what now-a-day we might call a Sabbath-school Picnic, the first of the kind perhaps ever held. The spot, selected on this

occasion, was on one of the Mendip hills, eight miles from
Cowslip Green, commanding a beautiful and varying prospect of the British channel and the Welsh mountains,
with quiet hamlets in the foreground: a spot of land was
fenced in, tents were pitched, and tables spread; children
and teachers flocked to the spot at an early hour; a large
party in wagons started from Cowslip Green, while the
strangeness of the event attracted innumerable lookers-on
without the enclosure. Psalms were prettily sung, perhaps
addresses were happily made, and nine hundred sat down
to a dinner of beef, plum pudding, and cider: all the
neighboring clergy were present, and grace was said at
each table; the day was fine, and Miss Patty's fears
speedily subsided before the good order and decorum
which everywhere prevailed throughout this immense
gathering. A general chorus of "God save the King"
closed the festivities of the day, Miss More ever inculcating
loyalty among the duties of religion.

The female clubs also had their anniversary days, when
the members heard a sermon at the parish church, and
then, adjourning to one of the school-rooms, prettily decorated for the occasion, with flowers and evergreens, tea and
cakes were served by Miss More and her sisters. These
feasts, which continued to be held, from time to time, were

attended with the most beneficial results, in arousing the self-respect of the poor, and creating a stronger sympathy in their behalf among those whose power it was to benefit.

A train of carriages, extending no less than a mile, frequently left Cowslip Green on such occasions, nor did the highest dignitaries in church or state disdain the thatched school-houses of Cheddar and Shipham.

On one pleasant summer's day, a gentleman came that way. " How beautiful is this !" he said to himself, stopping at the gate, to survey the rural charms of Cowslip Green.

Miss Mary More issued from the shrubbery, and with hospitable intent, invited the stranger to enter.

Delighted with the situation and garden, he inquired to whom it belonged.

" Miss Hannah More," was the reply of the eldest.

His surprise seemed only equal to his pleasure. An introduction followed, and Mr. Turner, for it was he, was willingly led to the house, where Hannah herself received her former lover with the utmost cordiality and kindness.

Their long-suspended intercourse was renewed, and remained unbroken until his death. He became a not unfrequent guest at the Cottage, and was the delighted spectator of the last picnic given by the ladies on the Mendip Ridge.

"Every cloud has a silver lining;" what may have been a source of disappointment and mortification to Miss More in her earlier days, led to a life of usefulness, at once so conspicuous and exalted, that her praise dwells upon every lip, and her example quickens and encourages every heart.

CHAPTER XI.

Will Chip and his Brethren.

THE angry clouds of revolution which swept over France during the last part of the last century, began to gather around and darken the English horizon. The fond hopes which had been awakened by the assembling of the States-general, and which had given an unwonted glow to all those who desired her freedom from the political and social evils which encumbered her, had long since been dissipated: in place of reform there was revolution; confusion and anarchy followed with swift and sudden step; opinions and principles hostile to order, government, and religion, were propagated under the guise of philosophy and fraternity, seducing the unwary by a promised good, which could never be fulfilled. The clubs of France had overturned and overturned, until the throne, the State, the church, all civil, social, and moral law had been trampled down, and the bleeding and stricken people were left to the reckless fury of leaders who knew not God, neither regarded man. Wild as was this spirit of reform, it swept over the English channel, driving from city to city, gathering up the loose and discordant elements of the English masses, threatening the peace of society, and the stability of the state.

As the agitation and discontent were beneath the surface, grumbling and muttering in the work-shops, the ale-houses, and the club-meetings, much of it was beyond the reach of statesmen, and below the cognizance of law: yet it needed to be met, met decidedly, yet naturally; met on its own grounds, with its own weapons,—English sense against French fraternity; tract and pamphlet against tract and pamphlet. Dr. Paley was enlisted in the service. He wrote " Reasons for Contentment," and a Prebend of St. Paul's was his reward. The book aimed above the mark: it relieved the anxiety of a higher class, but it did not quell the tumultuous hopes, or answer the dangerous sophistry of the discontented or seditious. Something more direct, more practical, more lively, was wanted; some-body with quick wit and sound sense, withal, who knew the men he had to deal with. At last, Will Chip showed himself to the English public. Will Chip, with no more, as it were, than a sling and a few smooth stones, ventured forth to meet the great Goliath of the times. Will Chip

makes no boasts : he simply asks to be heard and read,—
he has written " Village Politics," a tract, very brief, and
as everybody began to say, on reading it, very pertinent
and very pithy.   Bookseller Rivington issued it, and his
shop is thronged, for wonderful is the demand for " Village
Politics."   Bishops christen it, lords bless it, landholders
rejoice over it, everybody for law and order are thankful
for it ; it multiplies abundantly : one hundred thousand
copies are circulated through lanes and courts, entering the
shops, knocking at the doors, looking out the windows ;—
it speedily makes the circuit of the kingdom ;—it goes by
hosts into Scotland and Ireland ;—it leaps into France, and
passes into Italy,—it is hawked and peddled ; in hall and
cottage, " Village Politics" is known and read.   Will Chip
has proved himself a master-workman ; they say he is
thankful and contented, loyal and christian, with a plenty
to do, and a heart to do it.   " What is a French Demo-
crat," cries Will Chip, Jack Anvil the blacksmith being
his mouthpiece, " but one who likes to be governed by a
thousand tyrants, yet can't bear a king ?—and what is
French equality, but every man trying to pull down every
one that is above him, while instead of raising those below
him to his own level, he only makes use of them as steps
to raise himself to the place of those he has tumbled

down ?—and French philosophy, but to believe there is neither God or devil, heaven or hell ?—and French benevolence, but contempt of religion, aversion to justice, overturning of law, doubting all mankind in general, and hating everybody in particular ?—and as for equalization, fraternization, inviolability, it is nonsense, gibberish, downright hocus-pocus !"

Will Chip was certainly one of the most influential characters in all England,—he was a man for the time, and people say that his tact and intelligence did more than anything else to open the eyes of the masses to the follies of French politics, and set Englishmen considering that, "Though they had a king, he was so kept in, he could not hurt the people if he would ; that they had as much liberty as could make them happy, more trade and riches than allowed them to be good ; the best laws in the world, if they were more strictly enforced, and the best religion in the world, if it were but better followed."

Englishmen began to come to their senses, and see all Will Chip said was true. But who was this remarkable gentleman,—so shrewd, so pointed, so seasonable, so conversant with Village Politics and French policy ? Where did Will Chip live ? The Bishop of London knew, for he writes to Mrs. Chip :—

' I have this moment received your husband's Dialogue, and it is supremely excellent. I look upon Mr. Chip to be one of the finest writers of the age; this work alone will immortalize him ; and, what is better still, I trust it will help to immortalize the constitution. If the sale is as rapid as the book is good, Mr. Chip will get an immense income, and completely destroy all equality at once. How Jack Anvil and Tom Hod will *bear* this I know not, but I shall rejoice at Mr. Chip's elevation, and should be extremely glad at this moment to shake him by the hand, and ask him to take a family dinner with me. He is really a very fine fellow. I have kept your secret most religiously.

" Your very sincere and faithful
" B. LONDON."

But secrets, like murder, will out. Mrs. Boscawen has got at it.

"Oh, oh, say you so !" she writes to Hannah More. " It must have been *instinct* then that has made me send for a quarter of a hundred more of ' Will Chip,' and still for more and more; the last bale came in yesterday, and I see they will not last the week out; I had better have had a hundred at once. Last week I sent a packet to

Badminton, and my duchess answers me thus : 'We
have all read, and delight in your Village Politics.' A
gentleman here says he shall send for a gross of them to
distribute about in his neighborhood. I have not had a
gross, to be sure, like this Gloucestershire gentleman, but I
have had them past counting, little thinking—why, yes, I
did think, too, of somebody, though not just the true
body ; for you must know the first word I ever heard of
poor Tom Hod, or the sprightly consolations of his face-
tious neighbor Jack Anvil, was one night at Lady Cre-
morne's, where the Bishop of London pulled them out
of his pocket, and read the delectable dialogue to us, in
tones so suitable that he was interrupted continually with
our bursts of laughter (ask Mrs. Kennicott else, for she
was of the audience), and when he came to 'my lady,'
and sent her ' to cold water, and hot water, and salt
water, and fresh water,' he could not get on at all, we
laughed so immoderately. I suspected his lordship was
the author. ' Well,' as Tom says, I went home, and sure
enough I wrote upon a bit of paper that minute, ' a
quarter of a hundred of Will Chip, or Village Politics, to
be had at Rivington's,'—and this I gave to citizen Brown,
and bid him carry it early next morning to a certain
walking bookseller of mine, who procures me all the learn-

ing I deal in ; and this was accordingly done, but did not
hold me (as I said) three days—I have had many recruits
since, and must have more.   Last night a gentleman gave
me 'Reasons for Contentment,' by Archdeacon Paley, addressed to the laboring part of the British public.   I cast
my eyes over it, and though I honor Archdeacon Paley,
yet I assured the giver that I would send him the produc-
tion of one, the minute I got home, who understood the
language much better : and accordingly I despatched a
little packet of Will Chip before I sat down at home.   You
will believe that I have not forgotten to supply Richmond.
Our minister and our apothecary are supplied ; and the
first went to the house of Cambridge and there excited
envy, Mr. Cambridge declaring he wished he had written
it.   Mr. Rivington still dispenses them by thousands (I
hope some go to France), and though he cannot get
anything by them, nor the pleasant author, yet both will
allow that this is success."

It was a new department for Hannah More ; so useful,
so influential, so successful had she proved herself to be on
the side of government and order as a village politician,
that her excellent friend, the Bishop of London, besought
her to come out on the side of religion and the Bible in a
" Village Christianity."

15

The pen of Miss More was not idle. If French politics had alarmed and nerved her to action, the unblushing confessions of French infidelity shocked her moral sense, and filled her with the most serious apprehensions.

"What," exclaimed citizen Dupont, in an impassioned speech before the national convention in December 1792, "Thrones are overturned! Sceptres broken! Kings expire! and yet the altars of God remain!

"A single breath of enlightened reason will now be sufficient to make them disappear: and if humanity is under obligation to the French nation for the first of these benefits, the fall of Kings, can it be doubted that the French people, now sovereign, will be wise enough, in like manner, to overthrow those altars and those idols to which those Kings have hitherto made them subject? *Nature and Reason*, these ought to be the gods of man! These are my gods! Admire nature, cultivate reason! For myself, I honestly avow the conviction—I am an atheist!"

"Dupont's and Manuel's atheistical speeches," writes she in April to Horace Walpole, now Earl of Oxford, "have stuck in my throat all the winter; and I have been waiting for our Bishops and clergy to take some notice of them, but blasphemy and atheism have been allowed to become familiar to the minds of our common people, without any attempt being made to counteract the poison."

The attempt was however made by Miss More—" I know how paltry is the little I can do," she says, " but my conscience tells me that that little ought to be done."

Ah ! if every Christian were to act thus ! How many sit idly down to indulge in imaginary schemes of extended good, while smaller opportunities within their reach are neglected and despised ! how many excuse their sloth by pleading the smallness of their ability, or the inferiority of their trust !   Oh ! " *do* the little you can, for that little ought to be done."   God works through atoms ; the mightiest ministrations of nature are carried on by the simplest and humblest agencies, each doing its part in the universal plan.   There is a wonderful power in doing ; it enlarges your ability to do more ; it brightens the eye and braces the mind, and gives to life a double zest, and an unknown joy.

Miss More's " Remarks on the Speech of M. Dupont," made in the National Convention on Religion and Public Education, made its appearance in the spring, together with an address to the Ladies of Great Britain in behalf of the French emigrant clergy ; great numbers of those exiles were found in England, in extremely destitute circumstances, many lacking the comforts and even the necessaries of life. To those in Bath, the sisters freely extended the hospitalities of their house, and a thousand pounds were raised through Hannah's influence by the sale of her Remarks, and subscriptions raised by her appeal.

"Your work is so much above praise," writes Mrs. Montagu to her, "your mind so superior to vanity and a desire of fame, that I shall not repeat to you a word of the universal admiration it has excited, and the great approbation of the sentiments which prompted you to write it. I will barely assure you of what alone interests you, that this work will afford great assistance to the poor refugees, and will be of infinite service to the souls of thousands."

Thus in doing the little she could, because that little ought to be done, a stream of blessing gushes up where her steps have been.

The bleakness of this prospect, is relieved by a playful extract from a letter by the Bishop of London to the lady of Cowslip Green :—-

"As you certainly belong to my diocess, and are on many accounts fairly entitled to the benefit of clergy (for you can not only read, but also write, and even preach, to the great world more eloquently than most clergy-women),

I cannot do very much amiss, I think, in sending you the enclosed charge. There are two things at least, you will learn from it,—to sing psalms more melodiously in your parish-church, and to reside more constantly in your proper diocess, from which (as I know by experience) you are but too apt to wander, and to be led astray into the flowery paths of Cowslip, and suchlike seducing and dangerous places, where you forget, amid the dissipations of solitude, your duty towards your neighbor, and never think of bestowing one single solitary line on Mr. Walpole, or on me. I have lately received a letter from him, in which he complains most bitterly of your pertinacious silence. Pray let us hear soon how your cowslips, and daisies, and acacias go on, and how many tons of hay you have this year, for I take it for granted you are a great farmer.

"Your friend, Lord Oxford, and myself are, I believe, the only persons in the kingdom worthy of the hot weather,—the only true, genuine summer we have had for the last thirty years ; we both agreed that it was perfectly celestial, and that it was quite scandalous to huff it away as some people did. A few days before it arrived, all the world was complaining of the dreadfully cold north-east wind ; and in three days after the warmer weather came in, everybody was quarrelling with the heat, and sinking

15*

under the rays of the sun. Such is that consistent and contented thing called human nature. As to ourselves, we enjoyed with gratitude and delight this truly Italian but short-lived summer. We lived in Bishop's noble northern room all the day, and in the evening the meadows were our drawing-room: there our little lawn was as green as an emerald, and kept constantly cool with fresh breezes from the Thames, while every other field and garden in the kingdom was burned up, and brought actually to the color of a gravel-walk. Our little cottage was indeed quite delicious, and this summer alone has amply repaid me for all my trouble and expense."

Great as was the care and labor of superintending the Cheddar schools, Miss More still projected new plans for the improvement and elevation of the laboring classes. There was at that period a great lack of reading, sufficiently cheap, lively, and instructive, to be within the range of their means or tastes. Hannah More asked, " How can this deficiency in the smallest degree be made up ?" In the unsettled, discontented, and inquiring state of the English masses, how necessary to furnish them with the right sort of reading : if Will Chip had done such essential service by his sensible and judicious endeavors in Village Politics, might not Will Chip be found to labor with the same efficiency for temperance, for economy, for religion, for social stability, and moral improvement?

Miss More thought they could be found: at least the attempt was fairly worth making; thence sprung the plan of "The Cheap Repository," a publication to furnish a story, a ballad, and a tract for Sunday, every month, and to be in part sustained by subscription, in order to bring it within the means of the humblest cottager. The plan met with the warmest reception from Hannah's friends.

"Thank you a thousand times for your most ingenious plan," exclaimed the Earl of Oxford. "May great success reward you! How calm and comfortable must your slumbers be on the pillow of every day's good deeds!" The Bishop of London armed his extensive influence in its behalf, and when issued, his library table was always covered with this penny literature, in order to make it the subject of conversation with all new-comers. Patty and Sarah, with other friends, promised their assistance, and the work was happily commenced. Two committees were formed in London to promote its regular circulation, and two millions were sold the first year.

In the winter of the year 1794, which had been almost unremittingly occupied in work among her schools, with her pen, or in lesser schemes of active usefulness, she jour-

neyed to London, and paid a few visits among the halls
and haunts of wealth and leisure.

"Last Saturday I dined with Mrs. Montagu. It was almost two years since I had found myself in such *grande
monde;* so I told them if I should be caught doing anything vulgar, they must give me a jog. We were fourteen
at dinner, and many more were added after, most of them
my old and intimate friends, who seemed to receive me
with great kindness. I told them to make much of me,
for their opportunities of seeing such a rarity would be
few. Mrs. Montagu is well, bright, and in full song, and
had spread far and wide the fame of Cowslip Green, and
the day she passed there. In the midst of all the splendor
of lights, and grandeur, and luxury, word was brought in
of the death of poor Lady E——. It was a tremendous
warning : she was an amiable, generous, and charitable
woman, but was immersed in luxury and splendor.

"I went to Mrs. Boscawen, with whom I shall make a
point to pass all the time I can spare. We have had
many hours' quiet discussion. She is better, but I fear
breaking up.

"Three o'clock.—Called down to Mr. Henry Thornton,
just arrived from Clapham, where he, Mr. Wilberforce, and
Mr. Elliott have been quietly enjoying themselves several

days. We have had two or three hours' prate, but our spirits were not exhausted : he is not in very stout nealth. Yesterday I went to hear Mr. Cecil,—Naaman the Syrian —very excellent."

Brief records of herself, penned at this time, reveal the jealousy with which she watched her straying affections, lest the beautiful and attractive accomplishments of London life might seduce her from that watchfulness, steadfastness, and self-discipline, without which it is difficult, nay, impossible, to maintain the spirit and the essential traits of christian character.

March.—" Dined with friends at Mrs. —— What dost thou here, Elijah ? Felt too much pleased at the pleasure expressed by so many accomplished friends, on seeing me again. Keep me from contagion."

Sunday.—" I see the need of doing the duty of every day in *its* day. When I look back on the past week, I see cause of mourning over my vanity and folly. Sloth and self are getting strong dominion, and much time wasted, which I had devoted to improvement. Let these continual discoveries make me humble."

May.—" Came to Fulham to my dear bishop—much kindness—literary and elegant society ; but the habits of polished life, even of virtuous and pious people, are too relaxing. Much serious reading, but not a serious spirit; good health, with increased relaxation of mind; thus are the blessings of God turned against himself."

Some of Miss More's most capital efforts were in the pages of the Cheap Repository. The Shepherd of Salisbury Plain, originally one of the Sunday Tracts of this publication, alone will immortalize her, whose Mr. Johnson is the dear and early friend of the sisters, Sir James Stonehouse; and the Shepherd's humble cottage on Cherril Down, is still pointed to the traveller in quest of curious relics.

Her ballads obtained great favor and influence throughout the kingdom. In consequence of the political distractions of the Continent, and the war which England was called upon to wage, together with the extreme severity of the weather, in 1795, which cut off the crops, there was great suffering among the lower classes of the English people; cold, scarcity, and discontent everywhere prevailed to an unusual and alarming degree. The Cheap Repository, with wonderful sagacity, furnished plans and precepts for enabling the people to bear the ills which pressed so heavily upon them, and inculcated religious truths in so simple and direct a manner, that the faith of multitudes, alarmed by the plausible and shallow arguments of infidelity, became confirmed and strengthened in the good old ways of their fathers.

Numerous and illustrious was the race of Chips. Mrs. Jones' cheap dishes in "Hester Wilmot," were in repute even at the tables of the rich; "Black Giles the Poacher" frightened everybody trying to live by their wits, rather than their work; no temperance agent ever effected more good than "Sorrowful Sam," while the "Riot" ballad seasonably sung among a gang of miners on the eve of a rising, opened their eyes to the truth of Jack Anvil's eloquent appeal,

> " What a whimsey to think thus our bellies to fill,
> For we stop all the grinding by breaking the mill !
> What a whimsey to think we shall get more to eat
> By abusing the butchers who get us the meat !
> What a whimsey to think we shall mend our spare diet,
> By breeding disturbance, by murder and riot,"

saved the mills, spared the butchers, and restored quiet to a most seditious neighborhood.

Bishop Butler's Analogy for half-penny, is surely worthy of a record; the doubts, perplexities and sinful grumblings, of many a one careful and troubled about many things, are happily and sensibly rebuked in this most excellent epitome of one of the grand truths of God's providential government; indeed, no one can read "Turn the Carpet," without having his faith confirmed, and, whether he confess it or not, becoming more ashamed of envious comparisons and ungrateful murmurs than he ever was before.

TURN THE CARPET,

OR, THE TWO WEAVERS.

IN A DIALOGUE BETWEEN DICK AND JOHN.

As at their work two weavers sat,
Beguiling time with friendly chat;
They touch'd upon the price of meat,
So high, a weaver scarce could eat.

"What with my brats and sickly wife,"
Quoth Dick, "I'm almost tir'd of life:
So hard my work, so poor my fare,
'Tis more than mortal man can bear.

How glorious is the rich man's state!
His house so fine! his wealth so great!
Heav'n is unjust, you must agree,
Why all to him? why none to me?

In spite of what the Scripture teaches,
In spite of all the parson preaches,
This world (indeed I've thought so long)
Is rul'd, methinks, extremely wrong.

Where'er I look, howe'er I range,
'Tis all confus'd, and hard, and strange,
The good are troubled and oppress'd,
And all the wicked are the bless'd."

Quoth John: " Our ign'rance is the cause
Why thus we blame our Maker's laws;
Parts of his ways alone we know,
'Tis all that man can see below.

See'st thou that carpet, not half done,
Which thou, dear Dick, hast well begun?
Behold the wild confusion there,
So rude the mass it makes one stare!

A stranger, ign'rant of the trade,
Would say, no meaning's there convey'd;
For where's the middle, where's the border?
Thy carpet now is all disorder."

Quoth Dick, "My work is yet in bits,
But still in ev'ry part it fits;
Besides, you reason like a lout,
Why, man, that *carpet's inside out.*"

Says John, " Thou say'st the thing I mean,
And now I hope to cure thy spleen;
This world, which clouds thy soul with doubt,
Is but a carpet inside out.

16

As when we view these shreds and ends,
We know not what the whole intends ;
So when on earth things look but odd,
They're working still some scheme of God.

No plan, no pattern, can we trace,
All wants proportion, truth, and grace ;
The motley mixture we deride,
Nor see the beauteous upper side.

But when we reach that world of light,
And view those works of God aright,
Then shall we see the whole design,
And own the workman is divine.

What now seem random strokes, will there
All order and design appear ;
Then shall we praise what here we spurn'd
For then the *carpet shall be turn'd.*"

" Thou'rt right," quoth Dick, " no more I'll grumble
That this sad world's so strange a jumble ;
My impious doubts are put to flight,
For my own carpet sets me right."

CHAPTER XII.

Trials and Opposition.

In the leafy month of June, Wilberforce made a bridal journey to Cowslip Green; Miss More willingly abandoned the splendors of London, whither she annually went to visit a few of the old and well-beloved, to welcome the newly married. " By this coming," she says, " he prepaid a sort of vow, made many years since,—you will think it not amiss to make his agreeable wife set out with such an act of humility."

On the following Sunday, in company with the sisters, he visited the schools of Shipham, Axbridge, and Cheddar, the last of which particularly delighted him : Cheddar then was not the Cheddar of his first visit, eight years before, when the sight of its ignorant and wretched poor robbed him of the pleasure, which the beauties of the surrounding scenery might have otherwise afforded him. The Sabbath-school had been there, preaching its gospel of love, and waste homes and desolate hearts had begun to bud and blossom like the rose. Wilberforce rejoiced and thanked God for the blessed sight.

This year, 1797, had been marked by his marriage and the printing of his " Practical Christianity," for its publication had long been before the world, by his life, a living epistle, known and read by all men. Practical Christianity was then at a very low ebb; there was little or no demand for religious reading, and many of his friends tried to dissuade him from issuing a work of this kind.

"If you put your name to it, you may possibly sell five hundred copies," said his bookseller, looking as if he thought that extremely doubtful. But the hidden want of the times, widely felt, was yet little understood: a religious book of *its* nature and spirit was needed, and when it appeared, the supply met a demand, at least in the material, for in a few days it was out of print.

"I am truly thankful to Providence," says the excellent Bishop Porteus, " that a work of this nature has made its appearance at this tremendous moment. I pray God it may have a powerful and extensive influence upon the hearts of men, and in the first place upon my own, which is already humbled, and will, I trust, in time be sufficiently humbled by it." "Such a book at such a time, and by such a man !" exclaims Newton: "I accept it as a token of good, yea, as the brightest token I can discern in this dark and perilous day !"

Fifteen editions issued from the English press ; twenty-five were sold in this country, and it holds a high place among the instrumentalities that gave a quickened impulse to that warm and more earnest piety, which has distinguished the last half-century.

While Wilberforce visits Cowslip Green in person, to take sweet counsel with Hannah More, and to join the sisters in their walks of usefulness, Newton remains by the sheep of his pasture, enjoying their society and sympathy, as fancy sketches them in the quiet of his study, or along the dust and din of Cheapside. " I am gone to the Vale of Mendip," writes he, " to Cowslip Green, to the Root House, where perhaps the ladies are just now assembled to breakfast. Oh ! could I actually see them, with what glee should I say, ' Good morning, ladies !'

" Well, I must be content with ideal visits for the present, but not always : a day is approaching when we hope to have a joyful meeting indeed. I trust that Cowslip Green is holy ground, and all the inhabitants consecrated persons ; sprinkled, like the priests of old, with the atoning blood, anointed with the holy unction, and devoted with united hearts, hands, and tongues, to do the will and to proclaim

16*

the praise of our God and Saviour. It is no wonder that I so long to be with them.

"Indeed, I am with you in spirit, and I think this is more than a sally of the imagination; the communion of saints, which we profess to believe, like the communion of the members of the body, is derived from a communication of life and spirits from the same common Head, by which they have reciprocal fellowship and fellow-feeling among themselves: and though believers, the salt of the earth, are scattered up and down, far and wide, to preserve the whole mass from putrefaction, they are *one* in Him. The supreme object of their love is as yet unseen. For His sake they love all who love Him, though it is but few of them comparatively that they can expect to see, until He shall collect them together in the great day of His appearance. The virtue of the heavenly magnet, which draws them all to himself, connects them at the same time with each other. Their aims, their hopes, and their spiritual sustenance are the same. Local distance neither discourages their mutual prayers, nor prevents their efficacy.

"The shadows of evening are advancing upon me. If ever I see Mendip again, it must be by a bird's-eye view from the higher hill of Zion above. But I trust I shall, at intervals, recollect with pleasure, the happy week I passed at Cowslip Green, while I can remember anything."

The New Year's day of 1798 was solemnized by Hannah More, by a renewed and more entire dedication of herself to the service of her Heavenly Master. " Let me now give myself away with a more entire surrender than I have ever yet made," she records.

" 1st. I resolve, by the grace of God, to be more watchful over my temper.

" 2d. Not to speak rashly or harshly.

" 3d. To watch over my thoughts,—not to indulge in vain, idle, resentful, impatient, worldly imaginations.

" 4th. To strive after closer communion with God.

" 5th. To let no hour pass without lifting up my heart to him, through Christ.

" 6th. Not to let a day pass without some thought of death.

" 7th. To ask myself every night, when I lie down, am I fit to die?

" 8th. To labor to do and to suffer the whole will of God.

" 9th. To cure my over-anxiety, by casting myself on God, in Christ.

" I resolve to pray at least twice a week, separately, for

the country in this time of danger, independently of the petitions offered up in my other prayers.

"Lord, grant that my religious advantages may never appear against me.   Many temptations this week to vanity. Flattery without end.   God be praised, I was *not* flattered : twenty-four hours' headache makes me see the vanity of all this ! Am I tempted to vanity ? Let me recall to mind the shining friends I have lost this year,—eminent each in his different way, yet he that is least in the kingdom of heaven is greater than either."

Among these shining friends was Horace Walpole, whose twenty years of unclouded kindness and pleasant correspondence, Miss More could not give up without a sigh.

As the best evidence of the earnestness of her piety, we find her this year extending her labors, and establishing a new school at Wedmore, the largest parish in the county, and deplorably ignorant. In the undertaking, she met with unnumbered trials: the farmers were very angry with her interference, as they called it, and were more hostile than any which the sisters had before encountered ; in superintending her workmen in a damp and unfinished building, to be used as a school-house, she took a violent cold, which threw her upon a sick bed for several weeks.

Though harassed and opposed, she went bravely on : it was enough for her to know that the work was to be done, and that in Providence she seemed to have been the appointed workman.

Having partially recovered, Wilberforce came down from Bath, and carried her thither, to take the benefit of the waters, and to relieve her for a short time from the burden of her manifold labors.

"I feel it rather base to steal off and leave poor Patty to work double tides," she wrote to Mrs. Kennicott. "We have in hand a new and very laborious undertaking; but the object appeared to me so important that I did not feel myself at liberty to neglect it.

"The opposition I have met with, in endeavoring to establish an institution for the religious instruction of these people would excite your astonishment : in spite of it, however, which far exceeds anything which I have met with, I am building a house and taking up things on such a large scale, that you must not be surprised if I get into debt. Providence, I trust, will carry me through the undertaking; for, notwithstanding the active malevolence we experience, I have brought already three or four hundred under a course of instruction. The worst part of the story is, that thirty miles there and back is a little too much these short days; and when we get there our house has neither windows nor doors: but if we live till next summer, things will mend, and in so precarious a world as this is, a winter was not to be lost."

Let those, who now grumble over the unthankful task of Sabbath-school teaching, and willingly abandon it on the merest pretence or without any excuse at all, look at the arduous and unremitted labors of this heroic woman; here the work is laid out and you are solicited to engage in it, with all the various helps and advantages which Sabbath-school societies, papers, books, place within your reach, and the abundant encouragement, which fifty years' experience of their benefits can place before you.

How should her example make us blush for our languor and sloth in our Master's service.

Besides these active duties in well-doing, her pen had been busily employed in preparing "Strictures on Female Education," a work which appeared before the public in the beginning of the following year, and which abounds in sound and discriminating views.

It is again curious to observe how applicable to our own age are the admonitions and advice of fifty years ago. The tendencies then, as now, were towards amusement rather than sobriety, fashionable accomplishments instead

of valuable knowledge and practical industry, filial indepen-
dence in place of filial obedience.

The practical evils, which lie in the path of christian
education from low and imperfect notions of what should
be its chief aim, together with a false estimate of worldly
advantages, are portrayed with great vigor and truth.

Her pertinent question to the women of her own time,
may be asked with no less significance to ours, "Does it
seem to be the true end of education to make women,
dancers, singers, players, painters, actresses, sculptors, gil-
ders, varnishers, engravers, and embroiderers?

"*Most* men are commonly destined to some profession,
and their minds are consequently turned each to its respective object. Would it not be strange if they were
called out to exercise their profession or set up their trade,
with only a little general knowledge of the trades and
professions of all other men, and without any previous
definite application to their own peculiar calling? The
profession of ladies to which the bent of their instruction
should be turned, is that of daughters, wives, mothers and
mistresses of families. They should be, therefore, trained
with a view to these several conditions, and be furnished
with a stock of ideas and principles, and qualifications and
habits, ready to be applied and appropriated, as occasion

may demand, to each of these respective situations. For
though the arts which merely embellish must claim admiration, yet when a man of sense comes to marry, it is a
companion whom he wants, and not an artist. It is not
merely a creature who can paint, and play, and sing, and
draw, and dress, and dance; it is a being who can comfort
and counsel him; one who can reason and reflect, and feel
and judge, and discourse and discriminate; one who can
assist him in his affairs, lighten his cares, strengthen his
principles, and educate his children.

"Almost any ornamental acquirement is a good thing,
when it is not the *best* thing a woman has; and talents
are admirable, when not made to stand proxy for virtues."

May not much of the want of success, the failures, the
bankruptcy, the discouragements, the complaints of men
in business, be traced to a wrong domestic education?
Are not "The Times," out of joint as they may be, saddled
with more than justly belongs to them? Have not extravagant habits somewhat to bear? Are women sufficiently trained for a thorough understanding of their household duties? Do not fashionable accomplishments usurp
the place of domestic virtues? Turn which way we can,
gild and ornament, and reason and sentimentalize as we
may, life is life as it ever has been, full of practical evils,

unwrought materials, and sore trials, which require an earnest purpose, a patient, courageous heart, and skilful hands to meet them, to subdue them and to convert them into present benefit or future good.

Miss More's happy criticism upon the word "pleasant," it may not be amiss to introduce, for the benefit of many still among us, who are too apt to undervalue the greatest excellences of character, if their title to this quality be found wanting.

"There was a time when a variety of epithets were thought necessary to express various kinds of excellence, and when the different qualities of the mind were distinguished by appropriate and discriminating terms: when the words, venerable, learned, sagacious, profound, acute, pious, worthy, ingenious, valuable, elegant, agreeable, wise, or witty, were used as specific marks of distinct characters. But the legislators of fashion have of late years thought proper to comprise all merit in one established epithet; an epithet which, it must be confessed, is a very desirable one as far as it goes. This term is exclusively and indiscriminately applied wherever commendation is intended. The word *pleasant* now seems to combine and express all moral and intellectual excellence. Every individual, from the gravest professors of the gravest profession, down to

17

the trifler who is of no profession at all, must earn the epithet of pleasant or must be contented to be nothing; and must be consigned over to ridicule under the vulgar and inexpressive cant word of *bore*. This is the mortifying designation of many a respectable man, who, though of much worth and ability, cannot perhaps clearly make out his letters patent to the title of *pleasant*. For according to this modern classification there is no intermediate state, but all are comprised within the ample bounds of one or other of these two comprehensive terms."

Her chapter upon Children's Balls, which, she declares, are a triple conspiracy against the innocence, health, and happiness of children, would be likely to give almost as much offence now as it did then. The remark of a christian mother in one of our cities, " that the increasing prevalence of evening dancing parties, and late hours for young children, she could not consider but a serious evil, yet she felt she should be obliged to yield to the fashion, and suffer her girls to attend," revealed a sad defection in parental training, which it is to be feared is gaining ground in the religious community.

Are not pious parents too much disposed to yield to fashionable requirement at the expense of their religious principles and christian profession? Have we habitually and seriously in view the chief end, the main object, for which we *profess* to educate our childen ? alas, we fear not.

Our children *are* to be educated as immortals as well as mortals, for the service of God as well as citizens of the world ; while we regard their temporal good with deep interest, their eternal welfare must still occupy the largest share of our anxieties and efforts. Under the burden of joy, and of new responsibility at their birth, we hasten to present them before the Lord, and enter into covenant with Him for His grace to aid us in training them for his service ; their spiritual entrance into his kingdom, with the consequent fruits of a holy life, is the one great thing aimed at and agonized for by parental love. To effect this, a judicious religious education must be our chief concern. To guard the appetites and chasten the passions ; to make the conscience tender and the spirit teachable ; to impart correct tastes, to enable the young mind to form right judgments and firmly to act up to them ; rightly to instruct in the knowledge of God, and to take advantage of opportunities, when the ear is open, and the feelings are tender, to bring the young heart to its Saviour,—what a work is this, and what obstacles to oppose it ! How soon we perceive that the bias is everywhere downward : in the little bosom is the growth of evil passions, and the walls of the nursery cannot keep out the contagion of evil influence, fitted to cherish them: there are foes all about the heavenward path of the little pilgrim, and shall the parent become its enemy? Will you impart to your children tastes which must oppose an obstacle to a taste for religious duties and enjoyments? Will you deliberately train them to amusements which they must renounce to lead a life of piety? You may, at first, see no harm lurking in the graceful snares and joyful excitement of the first dance, but cannot you look still farther and see that you are thrusting the child of your love beyond the prayers of the church, and estranging it farther and farther from the influence of the Holy Spirit? And you do this by teaching it to love that amusement which most exposes it to frivolity and the spirit of a tempting and giddy world; an amusement which banishes habitual thoughtfulness, and produces a disrelish for the pure and peaceable exercises of a devout and humble life. Oh! christian parents, think of these things.

The "Strictures" were greatly commended; letters of thanks, congratulation, encouragement, and praise poured in upon the author, from the old circle, Mrs. Boscawen, Mrs. Montagu, Mrs. Chapone, Miss Carter, Mrs. Barbauld, and from many others less familiar to these pages.

The sisters, Hannah and Patty, now went up to London for the benefit of a change, to both mind and body. Mrs. Boscawen was extremely feeble at this time ;—"God bless you, my dear madam," said Hannah, on coming away, fearing it might be the last meeting.

"That is well," said the venerable lady, taking her by the hand, and looking steadfastly into her face, "that is well, but you must do more, you must pray for me,—I am going gently off."

Miss Carter, now at eighty-three, was in the enjoyment of better health and spirits than usually fall to the lot of so advanced age, and the conversation of the friends, if not as sparkling and witty, savored of christian hopes and holy joys.

Meanwhile troubles were brewing in one of the parishes where a school had been established, which, at the time, proved extremely vexatious and distressing to Miss More and her family ; viewed through the lapse of years, it seems strange that charges so utterly inconsistent with reason and fact could have been made against her, and that the affair could ever have assumed the dignity of a " controversy."

A school had been established in the profligate parish of Blagdon, near Cowslip Green, at the earnest and re-

17*

peated request of both curate and magistrate, for Miss
More, on their first application, felt that she had neither
strength nor means sufficient for any new undertaking:
having consented, she paid particular attention to its welfare, and in a few years had the satisfaction of knowing
that disorders, warrants, and indictments had almost entirely disappeared before the benign and beneficial influence
of her Sunday instruction. For five years affairs went
smoothly on, when one of her schoolmasters, named
Young, was charged, by the curate, Mr. Bere, with intro-
ducing Methodism into his school, which, so far as we can
learn, consisted in encouraging extemporaneous prayer, and
speaking upon religious experience in a little meeting of a
dozen poor neighbors for religious conversation: for this
irregularity, as it was regarded, Miss More, who was then
sick at Bath, gave him a timely reprimand, and the school
went quietly on. Whether owing to some private pique
or personal dislike, the curate was not to be so easily satisfied: he began to preach against the schools, and brought
up a new accusation against the schoolmaster, to the effect,
that he had prevented a young man from entering his service by defaming his character. The matter was referred
to the rector, Dr. Crossman, and afterwards to a local tribunal, the result of which was the dismissal of the school-

master, and the breaking up of the school. Miss More acquiesced for peace sake, though she could not approve what her judgment did not sanction. Young had been in her service for ten years, and his exemplary conduct and faithful discharge of duty had won her confidence, not to be shaken by a single instance of irregular proceeding (for it is to be supposed, he never asked the poor neighbors to make another prayer), or any general charges, which could not be fully sustained : she recommended him to the patrons of a large charitable institution near Dublin, who, not long afterwards, appointed him superintendent, the duties of which he fulfilled with credit to himself, and to the satisfaction of his employers.

Disbanding the school cost her many struggles, for she loved it with a mother's tenderness. " It is with no small concern I have to inform you that we shall meet no more in this place," she said in her parting address to the little flock who sat around her, with anxious looks and tearful eyes. " The Sunday-school, and the evening reading, the weekly school of industry, are all at an end. Before we part, it is but justice to you to declare that my sister and I have never had more comfort from the teachable and dutiful behavior of any children, nor more satisfaction from the sober and decent conduct of any parents, than we have ex-

perienced in this place. You will give the best evidence that
you have profited by our instructions, and those of your
master, by carrying the religion you have been taught on
Sunday into the business of the week, and the behavior of
your daily life. I shall hold that person's religious profession
very cheap indeed, who is not hereafter sober, peaceable,
industrious, and forgiving. Be diligent in your attendance
at church twice a day. Show that you fear God, by keeping his commandments and reverencing his ministers :
show that you 'know the King,' by submitting to all that
are in authority under him, especially to magistrates. Mr.
Young has proved himself, during eight years' service, an
honest and upright man, and an able and faithful schoolmaster. You are greatly indebted to him, and can reward
him in no other way but by living in such a manner as
shall be a credit to his instructions. He will continue in
this place, of which he is a parishioner, till he can settle himself elsewhere ; but I earnestly request that, though
you treat him as a kind friend and neighbor, you do not,
either by many or by few, resort to him for instruction.

"Young men ! let me exhort you to be sober-minded :
avoid the snares and corruptions of the world, against
which you have been so long guarded, and to which, at
your season of life, you will be so much exposed. My

young women! so long the objects of our tender care and concern! I commit you to the protection of God. He can, and I trust He will, raise up better friends than we have been to you. In any case He will Himself be your friend if you walk in the paths in which you have been trained. He will never leave you nor forsake you. As those hours on Sunday evenings which you have been accustomed to pass in this house are the seasons of the greatest dangers to your youth and ignorance, watch well, I beseech you, over yourselves. You are now furnished with Bibles; you have been taught to read and understand them; so that, if you now fall into sin, you will no longer have the former excuse of ignorance to plead. We have this day repeated our annual gift of forty Bibles and Common Prayer-books, the usual number of Bishop Gartrell's 'Institutes,' Bishop Beveridge's 'Private Thoughts,' Doddridge's 'Rise and Progress of Religion,' for the elder, with some hundreds of Cheap Repository and other small tracts, for younger ones. To the use of these you must add prayer to God for His grace and direction. Though what little we have done here is mixed with much imperfection, yet I trust the general design and tendency of it has been right.

" We shall never think of the five years that are past

without being thankful for what has been done, and without wishing we had done more and better. To the principal farmers and heads of the parish we are obliged for their approbation and countenance of the school, and their kindness to the master and mistress. Being willing to leave a last testimony of our regard to the poor, we have deposited in the hands of your respectable church-warden, five guineas, to be applied to a general subscription, in case the scarcity should make such a measure necessary, or otherwise to be disposed of at his direction and that of the vestry."

What a tender concern, what a generous interest is displayed in this brief farewell: no censure or blame issues from her lips, nothing that can encourage discord or rankle in the heart; it was a gospel of peace and good-will to the little community.

The Rector having afterwards learned that the breaches of discipline of which the schoolmaster had been accused had never been repeated after Miss More's reprimand, no other charges having been preferred against him, Dr. Cross-man, by the advice of the Bishop, dismissed Mr. Bere from the curacy, and requested Miss More to re-open the schools: this request was warmly seconded by her own affectionate interest in the little Blagdon flock, and accordingly she re-assembled them around her on the 25th of January, 1801.

Neither was the curate so easily to be got rid of; having committed no ecclesiastical or moral offence, he could not be deprived of his office, and there he remained at Blagdon, a thorn in the side of all Miss More's endeavors: to disarm his hostility, in August, she again closed the schools, never to re-open. The British Critic and Anti-Jacobin Review, lent their pages to this controversy, which continued to be carried on with the utmost bitterness and personal abuse. Miss More's labors, character, and religious views were violently assailed; she was accused of Jacobinism, disloyalty, Methodism, nay, of French infidelity, and farther still, one of her enemies publicly declared she had hired two men to shoot him, and that she had been concerned with Charlotte Corday in the assassination of Marat. A bill was posted up on the Blagdon turnpike, showing the lengths to which men may be carried by the angry heats of party, even to the utter disregard of all that is honorable or decent:—

"Just imported from Barbary by Baron Munckhausen a large collection of strange beasts, which the Baron has had the honor of exhibiting before the Bishop of London and his party with great applause, and may be seen at any

time of the day in a new-built Caravan at the sign of the
Green Cowslip, in the parish of Wrington, at thirteen and a
half pence each. The collection consists of five female savages (the Misses More) of the most desperate kind, one black
bear (Mr. Bere) which they wounded with a poisoned dart
while he was guarding his young ones."

Sharp and severe were these trials to the sisters, especially to Hannah and Patty, whose labors were already
crippled, and whose usefulness in the other parishes might
be seriously injured in future by the unscrupulous charges
and bitter satires of their adversaries.

Grieved and wounded to the quick, Hannah writes to
Wilberforce : " In Blagdon is 'still a voice heard, lamenta-
tion and mourning,' and at Cowslip 'Rachel is still weeping for her children, and refused to be comforted because
they are not' instructed. This heavy blow has almost
bowed me to the ground. It was only last night I began
to get a little sleep. My reason and my religion know
that it is permitted by that gracious Being, who uses
sometimes bad men for his instruments ; but reason and
religion do not operate much upon the nerves. I doubt
not but that He who can bring much real good out of
much seeming evil, will eventually turn this shocking
business to his glory. Though I knew that Bere and his

adherents had spread abroad the most flagitious reports
respecting my political and religious principles, yet I own
I was inexpressibly shocked the other night at Patty's
receiving from the Bishop of London, a most ambiguous
and alarming note, expressing the utmost terror on my
account, yet refusing to explain himself; saying if what
was reported were true, she would understand what he
meant. All we can collect from this obscure giving out,
what out of tenderness he seems to have half concealed, is,
that this *mock* trial has been fabricated by B——'s emissaries
into an official one, and that I am found guilty of sedition,
and, perhaps, taken up and sent to prison. Remember
this is mere surmise. Have you had any communication
with the Bishop of London, or have these strange reports
reached you ?

"I mean to re-read for the fiftieth time, your chapter on
the overvaluing of human estimation. I have perhaps
been too anxious on that head. Yet few people have cared
less about general opinion, except as it has attacked me in
that vital vulnerable part, on which one's usefulness depends.

"I have had a return of my complaint, and am still very
poorly. Patty behaves nobly, and only works the harder
for all these attacks ; she has been, in all this weather, on

18

a three days' mission to Wedmore, where things look very smiling : our persecutors have become our admirers, now they say they have seen our goings on, and that we are not methody people ; and that rich farmer who presented us at the visitation for teaching French principles, sends his own family to the school and the reading, both of which are very full ; but I greatly dread B——'s success at Blagdon will induce a second visit to Wedmore, where he first stirred up the opposition. My wounds are still fresh and raw, and want much wine and oil—this your kind letters never fail to administer, but I hope I strive to look for higher and better consolations ; and that these may be granted me, I am persuaded I have your prayers."

Again she writes, " Mr. Whalley has done himself great honor by writing a strong and very spirited state of the case to the Bishop, expressing his strong conviction of the moral benefit to the country from all my schools, his firm belief in the integrity of the Blagdon master, and describing at large his having witnessed, together with Dr. Maclaine, Mrs. Holroyd, and many other equally respectable testimonies, the conduct of the school for a whole Sunday, the practical and useful mode of instruction given them, and the regularity and good order of the parish. I own I did think his testimony would have been of use. But it was very coolly received. *The man had prayed extempore*—he *might be a Calvinist:* the *church was in danger.* My dear friend, I have prayed and struggled earnestly not to be quite subdued in my *mind*—but I cannot command my nerves, and though pretty well during the bustle of the day, yet I get such disturbed and agitated nights, that I could not answer for my lasting if the thing were to go on much longer; this is such a specimen of the state of religion, that *I*, too, really think the church *is* in danger, though in another and far more awful sense."

For three years the persecution continued with unabated violence, to which was added a distressing illness, which confined her to the house for seven months; but Hannah More had consolations, which the world could neither give, nor take away; she leaned upon an almighty arm.

"The calumnies are of too dreadful a nature to be borne," she exclaimed, "except from a full conviction that it is the will of God, who is pleased thus to exercise me for my purification. Who knows but in the final issue of things, I may have reason to think these bad men are my best friends, having never before tasted anything but dangerous prosperity or unmerited praise."

Hitherto we have only seen Hannah More borne on favoring gales; her London acquaintance rejoiced in her society and celebrity; fame and friends followed her to Cowslip Green; her home missionary labors, difficult and arduous as they had been, were crowned with success; her works ranked her among the revered and honored of England; prosperity, we know, is neither favorable to piety nor self-knowledge; but the hour of trial came, from those whose teeth were spears and arrows, and whose tongue a sharp sword. She bows to the chastening, and with the eye of faith, sees mercy in the rod.

"If it please God thus to put an end to my little (how little!) usefulness, I hope to be enabled to submit to his will, not only to submit to it, because I cannot help it, but to *acquiesce in* it, *because it is holy, just and good.*"

Here is the childlike submission of a true servant of God. Though her reputation, her character, her labors were seemingly at stake, no words of anger, of recrimination, or of sinful repining, issue from her lips. Conscious of her innocence as far as regards her fellow-men, she offers neither defence nor exculpation: her chief desire is spiritual improvement; an increased purity of heart and a more humble reliance upon the Lord her strength. When Dr. Beadon succeeded Dr. Moss to the see of Bath and Wells, she deemed it a duty to lay before him a plain statement of the matter, lest he might be led to disapprove of her schools, in which case, she must defer to his opinions and relinquish them altogether.

Her letter is plain, straightforward, and full of that candor and directness which so eminently characterized her writing.

" ' Blessed are ye when men revile and persecute you and say all manner of evil against you *falsely*,' and for ' my name's sake.' When I consider whose words are these," wrote Newton to his afflicted friend, " I am more disposed to congratulate than to condole with you, on the unjust and hard treatment that you have met with.

" Yet I do feel for you. These things are not joyous but grievous at the time ; it is *afterwards* that they yield the peaceable fruits of righteousness. Cheer up, my friend, tarry thou the Lord's leisure. Be strong, and he shall comfort thy heart."

Among the heavy and conflicting charges laid against Miss More in this controversy, were those of teaching Calvinism, sympathizing with the Methodists, and encouraging Dissenters. Though firmly attached to her church and to her state, and to church and state, Miss More was less a church woman than a Christian.

" *Bible* Christianity is what I love," said she, " that does

18*

not insist upon opinions indifferent in themselves—a Christianity practical and pure, which teaches holiness, humility, repentance, and faith in Christ : and which, after summing up all the evangelical graces, declares that the greatest of these is charity."

No better description than this could be given of her religious character : it grew out of large, intelligent, experimental views of *Bible* Christianity. No other Christianity but that which is drawn directly from the pure Word of God can give equal symmetry and comprehensiveness ; that can blend in such just proportion, the deepest self-abasement and the most trusting faith, with the greatest amount of usefulness and good works.

CHAPTER XIII.

Barley Wood.

VISITORS without number flocked to Cowslip Green, until Cowslip Green was quite too straitened for the fame and hospitality of its mistress. She now projected a new house, more ample and commodious, upon a swell of land half a mile from Wrington, commanding a wider sweep of hill and valley, of hamlet and green; the peculiar beauty of the situation led one of her friends to call it, " the gift of an all-wise Providence, to soothe her after all her troubles."

In the planning and planting of her grounds, Miss More hoped to regain that tranquillity of mind, and strength of body, which the rude and unprovoked assaults of her enemies had seriously impaired.

Barley Wood became her residence in 1801.

Hitherto the sisters had divided their time between Bath and Wrington : they now determined to give up the care

and expense of a divided dwelling and a bustling town,
and spend the remainder of their days at Barley Wood.

"Lord, grant that this prove a blessing to us all and
draw us nearer to Him," exclaims Hannah ; "make us
thankful that our lot has fallen in so pleasant a place, that
we have a goodly heritage, but let us not take up with so
poor a portion as this life, or anything in it."

Barcley Wood became a centre of no common interest.
If the eye delighted to linger on the distant landscape, the
garden soon offered scarcely inferior charms ; fruits and
blossoms dwelt in social sweetness,

> "Along its blushing borders, bright with dew,
> And in yon mingled wilderness of flowers,
> Fair-handed Spring unbosoms every grace."

Bright carnations, gay, spotted pinks, the daisy, primrose,
violet, break

> "On the charmed eye, and the delighted florist marks,
> With secret pride, the wonders of her hand."

Nor within is there a less pleasing diversity. Each sister
has her assigned place in the household. There sits Miss
Mary, already past sixty, plain in her manners, and pointed

in her speech; who allows herself no indulgences, or suffers no impropriety to pass without rebuke. Miss Mary
More we venture to say, is no favorite with pretenders of
any sort : she has a key to unlock their characters, which
no one likes the using. Here is the *wife* of Barley Wood,
as some call her, Miss Elizabeth, so gentle, so loving, full
of the milk of human kindness ; her presence, like a good
angel, is everywhere felt, regulating, smoothing, harmonizing, and her work-basket, like Dorcas', is fitted with coats
and garments for the poor.

Sally More is bright and intellectual, like Hannah.
Prosy More she was called by intimates, not, however, for
her dulness, but in distinction from Hannah, who was
named Poetry. Sarah wrote two novels in her early days,
and her original sayings were without number ; indeed,
they declared she was a living contradiction of Solomon's
position, there was nothing new under the sun.

Many of the tracts of the Cheap Repository issued from
her pen, and were read with lively interest. The star of
the sphere is Hannah : she is world-known now, and everybody comes to see her, some from curiosity, some for advice, some for friendship, some to be famous ; some to admire, some to envy. She is affable and accessible to all ;
there are lines of suffering upon her face, yet it is beaming

with benevolence; the pressure of sickness is often heavy,
but her elastic spirit seldom yields: she thinks, and plans,
and works, and reads, even on the sick bed.

Barley Wood was stored with comforts; these could
lighten and alleviate, but they could not ward off the infirmities of life. On her first entrance to her new home,
she was confined to her chamber, and, "This puts me in
mind," she says, "of the old remark, that the first spot of
earth of which Abraham took possession, in the land of
Promise, was a grave!"

Among the children of England, who were sporting in
her stately halls, or starving at her cottage doors, one little
girl there was, on whose fair head rested a nation's hopes,
and around whose bud of being clustered the manifold interests of a mighty empire. She found her way to the
heart of every English mother, and was remembered at
every household altar; wise men talked of her, and good
men prayed for her. Among the royal household there
was none dearer than she, for to the winsomeness of childhood were added the snares and prerogatives of a princely
birth.

To the loyal heart of Hannah More the education of
the Princess Charlotte could hardly fail to become a most
important subject. Nor is it surprising that the gifted
teacher in hall and cottage should have been solicited to

furnish from the rich stores of her experience, principles
and suggestions that might afford valuable helps to those
who had the charge of it.

With these views she wrote "Hints towards forming the
Character of a Young Princess," dedicated to Dr. Fisher,
Bishop of Exeter, who had just been appointed Preceptor
to the royal pupil. Copies were presented to the king and
queen, the prince and princess, who all alike bore testimony
to its excellence. Sir Alexander Johnson sent it to the
Rajah of —— to be translated into the Mahratta language,
for the use of his favorite daughter. Not having the
speedy introduction to this country as her other works had
done, she understood it was excluded by our republican
principles; when informed that it was actually in circulation, she was much gratified, exclaiming, "I have con-
quered America." Richard Rush, Esq., of Philadelphia,
wrote her that he saw in it full as much of what is elevated,
and more of what is practically useful than Telemachus,
and that he had intended his son should read Telemachus
through every year from sixteen to twenty. The Hints
would form a very good companion to accompany it.

On the 7th of January, 1804, among the particular
mercies which crowned her days, she enumerated, " Considerable restoration of my health and spirits, personal and

family comforts continued, family misfortunes averted, opportunities of doing some good, our schools continued,
kindness of friends, ability to enjoy my sweet place, escape
from the turbulent life of Bath, increased opportunities of
reading and retirement, for which she desires to have an
abiding and lively gratitude—though for all earthly blessings we should pray only with entire submission to the Divine will ; while in praying for spiritual blessings, no reserve, no caution, no limit is necessary.

"Lord, pour out the grace of thy Holy Spirit on me and
mine without measure; teach us to love Thee with *all* our
hearts, minds, souls, and strength, and to devote the remainder of our lives to thy service, and to the glory of our
Lord and Saviour, Jesus Christ."

This month closed her correspondence with Mrs. Boscawen, one among the first and most devoted of the
circle of London friends.

"Yes, my very excellent and dear friend," ran her last
letter, " I must send one word sooner or later, in return for
the kindest of letters, which was a cordial to me ; that one
word must express the truest gratitude for such remembrance, the most constant affection, and the sincerest satisfaction in the news of your better health ; so happily pro-

vided for by your own wisdom and activity, in removing from the vale below, and planting yourself so delightfully on a hill.

"I desire the continuance of your prayers for me, my dear friend. For, oh! what is it to live so long! It is, you will answer, the will of Him 'in whom we live, and move, and have our being.'

"Mrs. Carter was taken ill while dining with Mrs. Iremonger, but is better to-day. Adieu, my dear friend."

But the hand is soon still in death, and her spirit released from the sorrows and changes of a long and checkered life: forty volumes of the Port Royal authors were left to increase the library of her friend, and recall the memory of days long gone by

Sickness again visited Barley Wood, and for a year Miss More seemed hovering on the confines of the grave; it was a period of sorrowful suspense to every one who shared her friendship, or knew her worth: anxious inquiries were daily made at the gate, and prayers for her recovery ascended from many a humble roof; nor was this solicitude confined within the cottage homes which had been comforted by her bounty, and lighted by her instructions: every post brought letters of inquiry and sympathy from their numerous friends, and at last, their fears

19

were put to rest, by the grateful prospect of returning health.

Meanwhile good and ill are sowing joy and sorrow around other hearts and homes. Cheddar, their first love, has sustained a severe loss in the death of its excellent curate, and the faithful coadjutor of the sisters in their labors of love : his plain preaching and pious life had been greatly blessed to the people of his charge; from fifteen, in a few years, the church increased to one hundred and twenty, who gave diligent heed to maintain a conscience void of offence.

"You would weep over Cheddar," said Miss More to Wilberforce, who loved Cheddar also, "if you saw the change occasioned by the death of Drewitt; no resident minister, only a galloper from Wells on Sunday, to a twelve minutes' sermon—of course the meeting thins."

A blessed era in humanity approaches. The great object, to which Wilberforce had devoted the prime of his life and the strength of his manhood, was on the eve of completion. Slowly, and steadily had the cause of abolition gained upon the conscience of the English people; in spite of defeats, distrust, and discouragements without number, the spring of 1806 brought blossoms of hope with the promise of a golden issue. The London Committee, after

an interval of seven years, re-assembled in Palace-yard,
an array of evidence was ready at any moment to go
before the House of Lords, Wilberforce wrote a powerful
appeal to the English public upon the Slave-trade, and all
the agencies which could be brought to action were again
marshalled and concentrated for the approaching crisis.

On the 22d of February, the first reading of the bill
took place before the House of Lords : it was a night of
agitation and excitement, of fear and hope : the vote stood
72 to 28.

"Oh Lord, let me praise Thee with my whole heart !"
ejaculates Wilberforce.

The House of Commons is grappling with it on the 23d.

Men speak boldly for justice and humanity ; they are
in earnest, and who shall gainsay them ? The opposition
was feeble and loose.

One of the members called upon men that day, to
mark how much the rewards of virtue were superior to
those of ambition ; to contrast the feelings of Napoleon in
his greatness, with those of that honored individual who
should that night lay his head upon the pillow and remember that through his agency the Slave-trade was no
more. Every eye was directed towards Wilberforce, and a
sudden burst of applause rang through the house.

The vote stood 283 to 16. A month afterwards it came for a third reading before the House of Lords; two days afterwards, the Bill received the royal sanction and became a law.

"Oh, what thanks do I owe the Giver of all Good, for bringing me in his Gracious Providence to this great cause, which at length, after nineteen years of labor, is successful!" exclaims the master-spirit of this exulting scene.

"To speak of fame and glory to Mr. Wilberforce, would be to use language far beneath him," said Sir James Mackintosh, "but he will surely consider the effect of his triumph on the fruitfulness of his example. Who knows but the greater part of the benefit, which he has conferred upon the world, may not be the encouraging example that the exertions of virtue may be crowned with such splendid success? How precious is time! How noble and sacred is human nature, made capable of achieving such truly great exploits."

"What a promise of happiness does it bear to millions and hundreds of millions of our species!" wrote Mr. Stephens, the husband of Miss Wilberforce, to Hannah More, "and from what a load of odious guilt and shame does it deliver our country!"

We may well suppose it a day of rejoicing at Barley Wood, and especially within the sick chamber of her, who penned, nearly twenty years before,

> " What page of human annals can record
> A deed so bright as human rights restor'd ?
> Oh may that god-like deed, that shining page,
> Redeem *our* fame, and consecrate *our* age !
> And let this glory mark our favored shore,
> To curb *false freedom* and the *true* restore."

But the excellent Bishop Porteus, who with grateful joy beheld this triumph of a most righteous cause, and whose friendship and encouragement had been dew and sunshine to the spirit of Hannah More, was now gently passing away. After his eye had become dim and his natural force abated, he visited Barley Wood, and spent a few days in her society, a few days golden with the treasured experience of a long friendship.

Similarity of taste and character seems early to have drawn them together; she was a frequent guest at Fulham Palace, where his sweetness of temper, playful wit, and innocent cheerfulness delighted the society of his more intimate friends, while he exercised the functions of his

19*

high office with zeal and judgment, for the promotion of
true religion and the best interests of humanity.

A few weeks before his death, Miss More received from
him a short and hurried note, begging her intercession at
the Throne of Mercy for divine aid on a difficult duty
which devolved upon him : "My great hope and resource
is, what I have always had recourse to in such cases,
prayer—give me then your frequent and fervent prayers,
and I shall hope for that most powerful protection of a
Gracious Providence, which I am convinced has never
failed in similar cases"—the nature of the duty, he did
not unfold, but on the third day, she received the assurance
that Prayer had had its usual effect, and all was well.
How sublime a closing was this to his long and useful
life ! Just ready to lay aside his official robes for the
winding-sheet, a report reached him that a club had been
instituted under the patronage of the Prince of Wales,
whose sittings were· to be on Sunday ; a sacred and strict
observance of this holy day, the Bishop having always
considered of vital importance to the community and
church, this public desecration of it, by those in high
station, filled him with sorrow and alarm. Rallying his
wasted strength, he resolved to seek an audience with his
prince and having arrived at Carlton House, leaning on

the arms of his attendants, he was led into his presence, when in solemn and earnest language he besought him not to violate the sanctity of the Sabbath, and lend his example to that, which must end in corrupting the morals and degrading the church. The Prince heard and yielded; and the servant of God departed in peace: a few more days, and he entered upon a Sabbath of eternal rest. Miss More erected a cenotaph to his memory on her grounds at Barley Wood, bearing the inscription :—

TO

BEILBY PORTEUS,

LATE LORD BISHOP OF LONDON,

IN GRATEFUL MEMORY OF LONG AND FAITHFUL FRIENDSHIP.

H. M.

CHAPTER XIV.

Falling Leaves.

IN the summer of 1810 we find Miss More making a tour among some good and agreeable friends in Gloucester, reviving the friendships of earlier days, and adding many new ones to the already extended list.

"I have been visiting," she writes to Mrs. Kennicott, "the scenes where we used to gipsy, and traced many a spot where I had picked dry sticks to boil the tea-kettle, under a shady oak, or broiled a r utton-chop on knitting-needles. The companions of our h .rmless rambles are all gone."

Dead leaves are strewing her way, and long shadows hover among the mellow tints of autumn.

Mrs. Montagu, sprightly and beautiful even at fourscore, had gone, and a volume of her letters was already before the public : they were her first letters, facts of an early correspondence with the daughter of the Earl of Oxford, commenced when she was but eleven years. Her friend and intimate, Elizabeth Carter, lived only a year or two longer, surrounded by all that could make long life venerable and attractive, "honor, love, obedience, and troops of friends."

Miss More has passed threescore years of her pilgrimage, and more, and if there be an abatement of bodily vigor, there is no slackness of the spiritual energies, the hidden fires that glow within. In spite of tormenting bile," a burdensome correspondence, and almost incessant company, time and strength have not been wanting to write " Practical Piety," one of her favorite works in this country, and one which is far superior to many works of a kindred character that have superseded it. After describing what Christianity is as an internal principle, she thus unfolds its practical influence upon man, in relation to his fellows. " The love of God, as it is the only source of every right feeling and action, so it is the only principle which necessarily involves the love of our fellow-creatures. There is a love of partiality, but not of benevolence; of sensibility, but not of philanthropy; of friends and favorites, of parties and societies, but not of men collectively. It is true, we may and do, without this principle, relieve his distresses, but we do not bear with his faults. We may promote his fortune, but we do not forgive his offences; above all, we are not anxious for his immortal interests. We could not see him want, without pain, but we can see him sin with-

out emotion. We could not hear of a beggar perishing
at our door, without horror, but we can, without concern,
witness an acquaintance dying without repentance. Is it
not strange that we must participate something of the divine nature, before we can really love the human? It
seems to be an insensibility to sin, rather than want of benevolence to mankind, that makes us naturally pity their
temporal, and be careless of their spiritual wants : but
does not this very insensibility proceed from a want of love
to God ?"

This discriminating extract may, perhaps, help us to
form something like a correct estimate of what is sometimes called "sentimental benevolence," " the rose and pink
philanthropy," which every now and then blubbers over
human suffering, as if nobody knew or cared for it before.
Some think everything of it, and hope all things from it :
others rate it very low, calling it good for nothing. What
is it really worth ?

It really feels for the disorders which afflict humanity,
at least, while it lasts ; it really desires to relieve them,
and sets about reforming some of the external and more
prominent evils, in the hope that if they are cured, those
of lesser note will naturally flat away, and society, in the
end, will be righted. Sin is regarded as accidental, rather

than radical; an *excuse*, rather than a *cause;* poverty a penalty for wealth, rather than a consequence of idleness and unthrift; restraint, discipline, and punishment the inexorable decrees of the few, instead of the necessary safeguards for the many; reformation of institutions is more aimed at than regeneration of principles. But it is found to be a far more difficult and perplexing work than was counted for: it is like stopping the leaks of an old building with sand; it gets soon discouraged at the hopeless nature of its task; yet, unwilling to abandon it, still anxious to seem to do even when it knows not what to do, or where to begin, it runs to find fault with those who continue patiently laboring, because so much still remains to be done, and rail at their instruments without offering them better. The truth is, this philanthropy springs from the natural sensibilities and sympathies of the heart, which are amiable, rather than efficient; self-loving, rather than self-sacrificing; the parent of feeling, more than of principle; partaking more of the demagogue than the true patriot.

The disordered state of the world, it must be confessed, is painful and perplexing in the extreme: but the disease lies at the heart and in the core of society, and there is no love for man but that which springs from love to God, which is strong and faithful enough to work for his salvation. The maxims, motives, and aims which control man are wrong, and nothing but the reception of those principles which God has given in the gospel of his Son, can essentially improve his inward, or better his outward condition. While much, very much may be done to benefit and reform the institutions of society, evils still remain which admit of no cure, but which must be patiently borne; and it is surely far more difficult to bear each other's burden than to comfort with the promise of removing them. In attempting, then, to do any permanent good to our fellows, we must not only relieve their distresses, but amend their principles; not only promote their temporal welfare, but be careful for their immortal interests; not only excite their activity, but teach them submission; not only give them alms, but forgive their offences. To do this, you must be patient and pains-taking, continuing on, yet ever forbearing. You must lay your account with ingratitude and improvidence, disappointment and reproach. You must meet evils with manliness, and exigencies without fear or disheartening. You are to expend no unavailing sympathy, to utter no useless complaints, to offer no affected condolence, to make no false promises. Your duty is to *labor and to wait.* In order to do this, you must love your fellow-men, because Christ loves them; suffer for them, because He suffered for them; labor for them, because He died for them.

"Practical Piety" cannot be too highly recommended; it should be in every library, as well as in every heart: it is a book for our serious and thoughtful moments, when we desire to inquire calmly, and seek sincerely after that obedience which is "perfect and entire, wanting nothing." Its *expression* differs somewhat from religious works of a later growth; it contains no fervid appeals, no declamatory entreaties, no exaggerated or one-sided estimates, no startling phrases; it discourses earnestly of our duties and dangers as professed servants of God; it deals candidly and plainly, telling us what we are and what we must be; it shows that no superficial obedience can stand in place of an entire surrender of the whole man to the service of God; it allows no partial standard, or low estimate, or sluggish action in the christian life.

"Many are reformed," it tells us, "on human motives, many are only partially reformed; but those only who, as our great poet says, are '*reformed altogether*,' are *converted*. There is no complete reformation of the conduct effected without a revolution in the heart. Ceasing from some sins; retaining others in a less degree; or adopting such as are merely creditable; or flying from one sin to another,

20

or ceasing from the external act without any internal change of disposition, is not christian reformation. The natural bias must be changed. The actual offence will no more be pardoned than cured, if the inward corruption be not eradicated. To be 'alive unto God, through Jesus Christ,' must follow 'death unto sin.' There cannot be new aims and ends, where there is not a new principle to produce them."

"It is not casting a set of opinions into a mould and a set of duties into a system, which constitutes the christian religion. The circumference must have a centre, the body must have a soul, the performances must have a principle. Outward observances were wisely constituted to rouse our forgetfulness, to awaken our secular spirits, to call back our negligent hearts. They were designed to execute holy thoughts, to quicken us to holy deeds, but not to be used as equivalents to either.

"Nothing short of a uniform and stable principle, that fixedness in religion which directs a man in all his actions, aims, and pursuits, to *God as his ultimate end*, can give consistency to his character or tranquillity to his soul."

In speaking of the importance of correcting small faults and cherishing the minor virtues, these making up the sum of human character, it says, " The reason why what are called religious people often differ so little from others in small trials is, that instead of bringing religion to their aid in their lesser vexations, they either leave the disturbance to prey upon their minds or apply to false reliefs for its removal. Those who are rendered unhappy by frivolous troubles, seek comfort in frivolous enjoyments. But we should apply the same remedy to ordinary trials, as to great ones; for as small disquietudes spring from the same cause as great ones, namely, the uncertain and imperfect condition of human nature, so they require the same remedy. You would apply to religion on the loss of your child— apply to it on the loss of your temper. As no calamity is too great for the power of piety to mitigate, so none is too small to experience its beneficial results. Our behavior under the ordinary accidents of life form a characteristic distinction between different classes of Christians : the least advanced resort to religion on great occasions ; the deeper proficient resorts to it on all.

"An acquaintance with the nature of human evils and of their remedy, would check that spirit of complaint which so much abounds, and which often makes so little difference between those who profess religion and those who do not.

"If our duties are not great, they become important by

the constant demand that is made for them. They have
been called the 'small coin of human life,' and on their
perpetual and unobstructed circulation depends much of
the comfort and convenience of life. How few of us are
called to carry the gospel in distant lands!—but which
of us is not called every day to adorn its doctrines, by
gentleness, kindness, and forbearance ?"

Alas, is there not a sad want of *thoroughness* in our
religious character in these days ? Is our religion exercised
as it should be, in fostering our little virtues and subduing
our smaller faults ? Are not Christians too apt to rest in
the hope of their conversion, without evincing its reality by
practical piety ? Are we not apt to think the business of
religion done by a sluggish compliance with some of its
most obvious requirements ? We may frown upon immoralities, but do we cleanse the heart ? We subscribe to
associations for good, but is there not a secret satisfaction
that we can delegate our names to do that, which we
should be loth to do ourselves ? The cardinal doctrine of
some seems to be, that " union is power," and as a natural
consequence most of the great evils of the world will be
banished by the existence of Societies, without one's having
any direct responsibility in the matter; they have great
faith in resolutions and reports, and they love to attend

the anniversary meetings; it gratifies their benevolence to hear what good has been done in Patagonia and Siam. As for the great mass of sin, wretchedness, and guilt within and around them, the most that could be said of it, *there it is:* and they content themselves with thinking that Christianity will cure it, only give it time: it sometimes strikes them strangely enough, that within the very heart of the christian community there should be so much corruption, but it is only a running commentary upon the Bible, and the Bible, they know, contains an adequate remedy for it; not many Sabbaths before, perhaps, their hearts have burned at the preacher's glowing account of that redemption, which cometh through Jesus Christ, but who shall illustrate its excellences, bear its gracious messages, and dispense its blessed charities, it is not for *them* particularly to inquire; they go to church and pay the minister, the Bible Society will do the rest, or the city missionary,—they subscribe to both. To neighbors and acquaintance, they are friendly and courteous, wishing them well; to a certain extent, they are glad to hear of their success, and they pity them in misfortune; if they are not members of the church, they hope they will be, indeed they rather wonder that some of them are not, they surely seem fit for it, though it might confound them to describe

20*

the temper and spirit that should belong to the servants of God. In daily life they are troubled and anxious about many things: petty annoyances and small trials vex the spirit and disturb their peace; indecision and peevishness, vanity and trifling, not restrained and subdued by that power which can cleanse the heart as well as guide the steps, bring discredit upon higher duties and dishonor upon the christian name.

It is often said that the church is false to her trust: we are often surprised to find how imperfectly christianized even Christians are; piety seems sometimes to have lost its savor, nay, it is even whispered that Christianity is a failure. These are something more than the suggestions of unbelief or the excuses of the short-coming. Alas, is there not cause for doubts like these! and do they not mainly spring from a lack of *thoroughness* and *completeness* in christian character, a want of that practical and progressive piety, which unhappily distinguishes but comparatively few? but which, wherever it is found, is just what the Bible describes it, a *sober, righteous, holy* living, *light in darkness, salt,* preserving and purifying. We need to carry our Christianity more into our daily tempers and hourly occupations; it is more needed in the counting-room, the work-shop, the parlor and the kitchen; it is needed to make us more honest, just, patient, charitable, meek, peaceful, and of *good report;* we must allow it to restrain and temper our *whole* man; we must live it in all the minor acts as well as higher relations of life, that all around shall perceive its excellency and honor its divine author; we must show that it is not variable and capricious, governed by our circumstances or self-interest, but that it is steadfast, *governing us*, and moulding our character into a growing likeness to Jesus Christ our pattern. While it lends a helping hand to those numerous instrumentalities and manifold associations, which are used to extend the knowledge of true piety, it must not suffer them to usurp the place, personal responsibility, and individual faithfulness in the humbler sphere of daily influence. In a word, nothing is more wanted to give strength and stability to the churches, power and victory to the word of God, discouragement and defeat to essential errors and sinful systems, than *Practical Piety, steadfast, consistent, and progressive* among the people of God.

Its excessive strictness was made a matter of complaint among some of her religious friends.

"The *gospel* is strict," was her reply; "the cutting off a right hand, or the plucking out of a right eye, though only used as metaphors and illustrations, is surely more strict than anything I have said. The standard of religion should be always kept high: the very best of us are always sure to pull it down a good many pegs in our practice, but how much lower is the practice of those who fix a lower standard than the New Testament holds out ?"

But, cannot you write of Christianity in more general terms, like Addison and Johnson, and not dwell so much on the peculiar doctrines of the Bible, they said again.

" Much as I honor and love these," answered she, " their writings would have done a far wider and deeper good, had they not generalized religion so much. The soundness of Johnson's principles is incontestable, but he scarcely ever enters on any evangelical truth. Addison had a devout spirit, still he appears not to have entered into those deep views of evangelical truth, which abound in Pascal and Taylor, in Leighton and Hall ; and my regret is, that they did not dwell more on the *doctrines* of Christianity, and upon what distinguishes it from all religious systems as a *scheme* of *salvation.*"

Compare the influence of Johnson and Addison, as moralists and Christians, celebrated and world-read as they are, with Baxter and Doddridge, how do they sink into comparative insignificance before the pungent, searching, humbling teachings of believing men, who took the Bible as God gave it, daring neither to lessen nor to narrow its solemn and awful truths, as they stand recorded on its inspired pages. It is such men only who can meet the wants of sinful man; it is only such preaching and such teaching that can measure the depth of human frailty and corruption, and which can propose a remedy to satisfy the conscious need of the burdened spirit. Men are frail, and imperfect, and sorrowful, but they are something more,— they are *sinners*, and are conscious of a weight of ill-desert, of which no one can relieve them. Christian generalities may arrest the ear, and please the reason, but they do not, and they *cannot* strike the conscience, compel a man to stop, let go his hold on the world, and cry out with an earnestness never felt before, " What shall I do to be saved ?"

It is only the distinguishing doctrines of the Bible, urged by those who have felt their power, that can have any direct or permanent influence upon the life and conscience of others ; any system short of a recognition of a man's apostasy, his pardon and restoration through Jesus Christ, with the consequent fruits of a holy life, all the tremendous issues of which hang upon immediate action, any system short of this, may it not be repeated, is inoperative and inefficient towards bringing men to repent ance and faith, to holiness and heaven. Believers there are all over the church of Christ on earth, who, under God, bless Doddridge and Baxter for the joy set before them, while saints, singing the song of Moses and the Lamb, will be crowns of their rejoicing in the Great Day.

It was this solemn persuasion of the essential features of Bible truth which gave such power to the teaching and example of Hannah More ; a power which offended some, but benefited more. In all her writings, and in all her plans for human good, her great and especial design was to *seek* and to *save those who are lost.* This was her heart's desire, and it was this which quickened her in her long and wearisome journey among the neighboring parishes, even after the infirmities of age and sickness crept over the body, and gave vigor to her pen, while the hand that held it was cramped with pain, and benumbed by weakness.

The earnest and heart-felt piety which springs from a believing reception of divine truth is often confounded with gloom and austerity, and yet there is none which can give such cheerfulness to life, and such hope in death. To one who asked whether her serious pursuits had not destroyed her relish for pleasantry, she replied, " As you cannot see those who live with me, you must take my testimony, that am neither a bigot nor a misanthrope,—my spirits are good, and even gay. I hope it is no infringement on better things to say, that my bite for humor, and a sort of sensible nonsense, is not a whit diminished. A life of ill-health has no ways impaired my constitutional cheerfulness, and I am sometimes afraid that I take more than my share of society."

Practical Piety was followed by Christian Morals, which soon passed through eleven editions.

But while her pen was more busy and instructive than ever, the sisters were compelled to curtail their labors on the Sabbath. The Mendip schools had survived the Blagdon controversy, and, like good children of a healthy stock, they looked well and thriving; neither spite nor misrepresentation could essentially, or for any length of time, impair an influence like theirs; but neither Hannah nor Patty were longer equal to the fatigue of superintending so large a field; three parishes only continued to share their benefactions, Shipham, Nailsea, and Cheddar, their last, as well as their first love. Here were teachers who had been twenty years in their service, faithful and well-approved; men and women, husbands and wives, and heads of families, who from little children had grown up in the schools, and become worthy citizens, and servants of God: many had

passed through sickness and tribulation, having obtained a
good report through faith, and at last died ripe with
christian hopes : peace, good order, industry, everywhere
prevailed over the once abandoned district ; friendly neigh-
borhoods and happy families, thankful hearts and tidy
hearths, bore witness that the word of God is valuable for
the life that now is, as well as that which is to come.

Now there is sorrow in Barley Wood : they who have
comforted others, need themselves comfort. Mary, the
first-born of the sisters, is not, for God took her : during
five days of suffering no murmur or complaint escaped
her lips ; calmly she talked of " going home," and picked
out the poor man who should bear her to her narrow cell.
The sisters gathered around her dying bed : it was Sunday
morning when she breathed her last.

" How blessed to die on Easter Sunday," spake Hannah,
" to descend to the wave when Jesus triumphed over it."

Twenty times a day did they visit her cold remains : " I
divide the morning between the contemplation of her
serene countenance and my favorite, Baxter's Saint's Rest,"
said Hannah, her tears stayed, as with the eye of faith
she beholds the eldest, " not lost, but gone before."

This was in April, 1813.

As the summer came, with its fruits and flowers, a journey, with its change of scene and air, was necessary to re-cruit the exhausted strength of the two younger sisters. They went into Surrey and Kent, drove through the environs of London, visited Henry Thornton, and passed a day with Wilberforce, whom they had not seen for some years, the home influences of whose quiet, but elegant house, greatly gratified Miss Hannah More.

" What extensive good has Mr. Wilberforce done among young persons of fashion, by the intellectual and religious intercourse of his family !" she declares. It was not only in his public acts and outward life that Wilberforce was a Christian ; in the bosom of his family, in his intercourse with his children, in the frank and chastened courtesy of his manners in daily life, everything revealed an elevated tone of piety.

" A few such hours," said she, " where inquiring minds know that they shall meet with good company, in the best sense of the word, would, I am sure, fortify the minds, and cheer the spirits, as well as confirm the principles of many. I know that many have been deterred from the society of religious persons by some want of discretion and delicacy, which they have been glad to magnify, in order to get quite out of the connection : I am, however, aware, that all one's prudence is not sufficient to clear away the charge

21

of enthusiasm which the world is ever watching for an occasion to bring forward against those who exhibit a more than ordinary degree of strictness,—but this they must be contented to bear for their *Great Master*, who bore so much for them."

But a great improvement was already visible in the higher class of English society : "Twenty years ago," said Jane Porter, "while a child, I have cried to hear people at the table scoff so at religion, with nobody daring to defend it : now such a thing would not be tolerated."

An increasing seriousness and respect for religious things were everywhere manifest; the Sabbath was more strictly observed : scoffing and levity upon sacred truths, were not only considered vulgar, but undignified and frowned upon. A higher and better tone of moral feeling began to pervade the public prints, and the tendency among all classes seemed to be upward : no small part of this change may be traced to the influence of Hannah More, whose literary fame preceded and opened the way for her religious writings. Known and admired as she had been in the most elegant and learned circles of the metropolis, it happily became the fashion to read her productions, and thus her works had an entrance and an unconscious influence in circles otherwise adverse to religious reading of so

decided a character, and indeed, to religious reading of any
kind. Nor did fashion here show her usual fickleness:
Miss More continued to be read and re-read, published and
circulated, with an ever-increasing interest and improvement ; nor can we ever imagine the time to be, when the
Shepherd of Salisbury Plain shall not be reckoned among
the most beautiful, touching, and truthful illustrations of
the power of divine grace.

But while our pen records her worth, she has left the
mansion of Wilberforce, and taken her way to Strawberry
Hill, now the residence of Lady Waldegrave, where a
thousand recollections of the past, partly pleasing, but
more painful, filled her heart. Here too was Hampton,
where for thirty years she had passed a portion of every
winter with Mrs. Garrick. It had now been several years
since they had met. Of all the old circle who first welcomed her to London, Mrs. Garrick alone was living, and
she was past ninety. Miss More hastened to see her ; she
was away, but the library, the lawn, the temple of Shakspeare—she would see all for the last time ! Contrast her
feelings now with the glow of youthful enthusiasm which
lighted her soul, and quickened her step, as she ran over
the lawn, and stood in the temple forty years before.
Youth and health were then hers ; life, sportive, gay,

literary, intellectual, was full of present gladness and future
promise. What blossoms of hope hung in her path! but
how little did she foresee or dream what the fruit should
be: forty years of summer and winter, of spring-time and
harvest; how many circles broken, how many graves are
grass-grown. "What wit, what talents, what vivacity,
what friendship have I enjoyed in this place," she said
tearfully. "Where are they now? I have been mercifully
spared to see the vanity and emptiness of everything that
is not connected with eternity; and seeing this, how heavy
will my condemnation be, if I do not lay it to heart."

Her frame is feeble, her step is tottering, her face
wrinkled with age; the air is chilly. So the outward
perisheth, but within, what a fountain of life! how price-
less, how exhaustless! What spiritual excellency, what
strength, what vigor, what serenity, what power beneath
that sinking and sickly frame! It is the divine life, drawn
from Christ, the living head.

The travellers returned to Barley Wood, and in the
autumn, Mr. Wilberforce, with his wife and daughters,
spent a few delightful days at this "favored seat of intellectual and religious sunshine," as it was afterwards
called by one of the sons of this favored guest. A new
source of interest and activity opened upon the sisters by

the formation of a Branch Bible Society, in the parish of Wrington. The great difficulty in obtaining anything like an adequate supply of Bibles for either home or foreign circulation, led to the foundation of the Foreign Bible Society as early as 1803, in which all religious parties united, alike without regard to party or sect. No society ever had a broader or more blessed mission; its operations were confined to no creed or country: its field was the world. When a few used to meet in Mr. Hardcastle's counting-room, to consult together and prepare measures for its formation, Mr. Wilberforce came also. It was planted a very little seed; it grew up and "became a goodly tree, which yielded her fruit every month, and the leaves of the tree were for the healing of the nations."

The first anniversary of the Wrington Branch, was held on the grounds of Barley Wood; the spiritual climate being cold, none of the Mendip gentry were sufficiently warmed with the subject to open their mansions. The meeting was held in the wagon-yard—one hundred sat down to dinner, and as it was a fine day, the overflowings from the house dined under the trees.

"Some may think it would have been better to add £20 to our subscription," said Miss More to Wilberforce, " and save ourselves so much trouble; but we take this trouble from a conviction of the contrary. The many young persons of fortune present, by assisting in this little festivity, will learn to connect the idea of innocent cheerfulness with that of religious societies, and 'may go and do likewise.' For no other cause on earth would we encounter so much fatigue." They all enjoyed themselves exceedingly, and the lawn had all the gaiety of a public garden.

Let us hear how Barley Wood and its gifted mistress strikes a stranger from the West. A lady from Massachusetts pays her a visit. "How did she look?"—and "what did Hannah More say?"—are fair questions enough.

"Miss More was about seventy-five years old, at the time I saw her, with an eye as brilliant as a girl of eighteen—a dark hazel color, with a full, matronly form of medium height. Her dress was of black cambric, with a plain, double muslin handkerchief over it, and a full-ruffled muslin cap. But her conversation!—*that* was the charm! interspersed frequently with quotations from Scripture. When we commended her works, and told her we thought great good had been done by them in America, her reply was, 'Oh, if *any* good has been done by them, if the few tinsel talents I possess *may* have been made useful! The Lord is sometimes pleased to employ the feeblest instruments in his service—do not *praise me*, but give God the glory, it is *all* of *Him!* You are very encouraging, and I need encouragement.'

" Miss More said, ' We might think it an odd speech she was about to make, but that we (the clergyman and his wife who accompanied me) could scarcely have found a day in many years, when they were situated as they were to-day. The Bristol Fair is now held, but we do not approve of fairs, and never allow our servants to go,— Bonaparte's carriage, however, has been a matter of great curiosity in this family, and one of my sisters has gone with four of our servants (for we dare not trust them alone) to gratify their innocent, though ridiculous curiosity, and you must receive it as a particular mark of friendship (at the same time taking Mrs. T.'s hand) if we ask you to take a bit of boiled beef with us—but we must wait on ourselves, and if, under such circumstances, you will partake with us, we shall be happy to have you.'

" On our fearing that to *dine* with them would detain us too long, she kindly said we must take some refreshment. She gave us cold mutton, sliced with bread and butter, and beer, all excellent. In the time it was preparing, we went over her cottage, which is neatly elegant, having a beautiful verandah in front, ornamented with a variety of flowers, and rose-trees, in bloom, rising even to the *thatched* roof, which covers this interesting dwelling. She showed us into a 'chamber for a friend,' commanding a prospect of the whole of Wrington valley, in which are situated twelve parish churches, and was the birth-place of John Locke, to whose memory she has a monument in her garden. Further west may be seen two islands in the sea, about nine miles from the shore, and she observed that 'their nearest market-town in the same direction is Boston ; so,' said she, ' when you reach home, look east-ward, and think of me.'

" Miss More told us the place was much endeared to them, from the circumstance of their having planted every tree, and shrub, and even laid the first stone for building their cottage, about thirteen years before, with their own hands.

" She took us to her bed-room, which is also a library, and pointed out the excellencies of almost every author, as we passed them, as familiarly as a parent could the differ-ent traits of her children. Baxter and Saurin were her favorite authors. She admired the sublime words of Bax-ter on his death-bed, when asked by a friend how he was, he replied, opening his eyes, ' Almost well !' meaning he should soon be with Christ in Heaven.

"Miss More was not well enough to walk with us over her grounds, but on our return to the house, we enjoyed her delightful discourse a little longer in the drawing-room.

"She said much of the evils of hoarding up wealth, and mentioned the death of a friend the previous week, by the name of Renolds, who gave away his immense property, restricting himself to bare necessaries.

"'Indeed,' said she, 'an avaricious professor of religion, is an anomaly that I cannot understand.'

"Mr. T. said it was a subject on which he should preach from his own pulpit, when he returned home.

"'Do,' said Miss More, 'and take for your text, But thou, O man of God, flee these things, Timothy iv. 11th, and think of me.'

"Miss More mentioned 'good news from India'—that a Bishop had written that he was then on the sea, going to another part of his diocese, which was five thousand miles in extent, and that a Bramin of high caste was lately converted, entirely by his own study of the Scriptures ('and yet it is said,' she remarked, 'this alone is of no use'), and that he, with more than two hundred of his caste, were soon to be baptized, when he intended coming to Europe, to a university.

"Her sister remarked 'that the evening before, Lord

Tinmouth and the Bishop of Gloucester had visited them, and that they had sat conversing until three o'clock in the morning, and all the time the words went as rapidly from one to the other, as the bird of a battle-door.' "

Is not this a pleasant visit? Can we not almost see the Lady of the Manor in her black cambric dress, and full ruffled cap? But, oh, to hear her!

Meanwhile Miss More was ready to issue another work, an essay to the Life and Writings of St. Paul—the first edition of which sold the first day, and she has not a single copy to present to her sisters. It is a discriminating and beautiful portrait of this eminent apostle, whose writings she had studied with profound interest. Three years had scarcely passed since the first breach in the family circle, when Elizabeth, or Betty, as she was familiarly called, followed her sister to the heavenly land. For many years, the Bible had formed her chief reading, and although a natural reserve prevented her from speaking with freedom of her interior life, yet

> " When faith and love, which parted from her never,
> Had ripen'd her just soul to dwell with God,
> Meekly did she resign this earthly load,
> Of death, called life, which us from life doth sever."

While her works, her alms, and all her good endeavors
were a rich legacy left in the memory of her friends, to
recall her worth. Her loss was serious to the family at
Barley Wood, for although her influence was chiefly felt
in the interior arrangement of the household, no one who
understands how many wheels there are within a wheel,
which need to be kept in harmonious action for a well-
regulated household, could undervalue the importance of
her position. Of diligent hand and pleasant memory, a
large circle mourned her loss.

The year 1816 and thereabouts, witnessed scarcity, de-
pression of business, and murmuring among the English
people. War had burdened the treasury, and crippled the
resources of the nation, nor could the proclamation of
peace immediately restore that prosperity and well-ordered
industry, which are among her chief blessings. Discontent
began everywhere to prevail; hungry men cried out for
reform; secret assemblies were holden; unpopular ministers were insulted; pikes were manufactured, and worse
than all, the agitation and violence of the times were
increased, by the circulation of a fresh batch of infidel
writings, adding fuel to the flame. The London committees
are again in motion: measures must be taken to circulate
throughout the veins and arteries of society pure blood, or

the whole will be corrupted by the bad. Among the publications of the day, Miss More's tracts and songs again play a distinguished part. Will Chip re-appeared upon the stage; "Village Disputants," the title having been slightly altered, rapidly ran through ten editions. Her quiet insight of just what was necessary, her true woman's tact, which serves the sex so well, often enabling them to reach the justest conclusions, without a troublesome argument, caused a fresh demand upon her pen at this time.

"I did not think of turning ballad-monger in my old age," she says, "but the strong and urgent representations which I have had from the highest quarters of the alarming temper of the times, and the spirit of revolution which shows itself more or less in all the manufacturing towns, led me to undertake as a duty, a task I would gladly have avoided."

She set herself to work, and in a few weeks, wrote a dozen penny and half-penny articles, thousands and tens of thousands of which were circulated far and wide.

"I fear the antidotes are not strong enough to expel the deeply-rooted poison," she says, "but each must do what he can."

"These are awful times, and this tempestuous weather, by putting a stop to the sowing of corn, I fear is preparing for us another season of scarcity. But *the Lord God* omnipotent reigneth ; what consolation to be assured of this !"

Are not here the grand elements of patient, earnest doing in the Master's work ? Every Christian who understands his relation to God and his fellow-men (and who dares profess ignorance in this day ?) understands also that he has a *life-work* before him, to do which, great as the work may seem, two simple elements alone are necessary, —*do what you can in the steady belief that God is at the helm.* He demands your service, and you need his direction.

Miss More wrote and published, and re-published many of her former tracts and stories, suited to the present exigencies, while her hand was weak, and her heart was aching to behold the slow and sure decay of her sister Sally, whose sprightliness and wit sparkled even amid the gathering ills of a closing life. For many months she knew there was no prospect of recovery, neither could any alleviation of the disease (dropsy) be hoped for, and she looked earnestly upward for those consolations which God alone can confer upon the soul in its hour of extremest need. While still below her sufferings were sometimes intense, which drew forth the frequent exclamation, " Poor

22

Sally, you are in dreadful pain." " I am indeed, but it is well," was her calm reply. Indeed, so much did she enjoy the society of her friends, so playful still was her conversation, so quiet and patient her appearance, that few could believe her situation dangerous.

Though yet able to stay in the family sitting-room, and employ herself a little with her work-basket, she gave up her old seat at the bow-window, where she loved to sit and watch the spring-flowers, lest the beauties of the earthly scene might draw her away from the frequent contemplation of the heavenly. At last, no longer able to bear a sitting posture, she was assisted up stairs—for the last time, she well knew: before leaving she looked back, and cast a parting glance about the room: it was a silent and solemn farewell: no word was spoken. Her sufferings greatly increased, so that with difficulty she could restrain the most piercing groans: unable to hear any connected reading, Hannah and Patty repeated detached verses from the Bible, in which she often joined. Once, when she had lain long insensible, a favorite text was recited, when she suddenly exclaimed, " Can anything be finer than that! it makes one's face shine!"

When life seemed nearly gone, her physician took her by the hand, and bade her good-morning: lifting her hands in holy transport, she said, "Oh! for the glorious morning of the resurrection! but there are some gray clouds between."

Her ejaculations all betokened a trusting and believing heart. "Oh! the blood of Christ! He died for me! God was man! Talk of the cross, the precious cross, the King of Love!"

"Blessed Jesus" were the last words which dwelt upon her lips. "Four months," writes Hannah to Mrs. Kennicott, "we have watched over her increasing disease. Poor Patty and I watched over this bed of suffering, but our distress was mingled with much consolation. I cannot do justice to her humility, her patience, her submission. It was sometimes more than resignation, it was a spiritual triumph over the suffering of her tormented body. She often said, ' I have never prayed for recovery, but pardon. I do not fear death, but sin.'

"My three sisters have quitted the world in the same order of succession as they entered it. My turn, in course, would be next. Pray for me that I may *do* and *suffer* the whole will of God."

A friend who visited Barley Wood after the last sad bereavement, writes thus of the remaining two sisters: "Feeling as they do, very deeply, the sad breach made in

their circle, they are wisely, cheerfully, and piously sub-
missive to this appointment of Providence : and neither
their talents nor their vivacity are in the least subdued.　I
am disposed to believe that they will be blessed to the last
with the retention of those faculties which they have employed so well.　With Patty I had a long .and interesting
conversation.　This interesting woman is suffering with exemplary patience the greatest pain : not a murmur escapes
her, though at night especially groans and cries are inevitably extorted, and the moment after the paroxysm, she is
ready to resume with full interest and animation, whatever
may have been the subject of conversation.　Hannah is
still herself.　She took the Rev. Charles Forster and me to
drive to Brockley Combe : in the course of which her
anecdotes, her wit, her powers of criticism, and her admirable talent at recitation, had ample scope."

How serene and beautiful is this picture !　We forget
that old age and sickness are there,—old age and sickness
so repulsive to the eye of blooming and buoyant youth,
so uninteresting and unattractive to the b isy and bustling
of middle life.　Hannah is seventy-three, and Patty is an
invalid, so, when Sally died, who cared for the flowers,
" The garden will be neglected," said some, " there is no
one left to do like Sally !"　Ah ! no : Hannah went out to

meet the spring flowers ; she gathered the : oses and bound up the honeysuckles, and the garden bloomed as sweetly as it used to : so the soul sometimes seems to renew its youth.

22*

CHAPTER XV.

Golden Harvest.

MISS MORE sits at her desk correcting the fifteenth edition of Celebs, and the eleventh of Practical Piety. She speaks thus, "In spite of the dull task of reforming points and particles, I found the revisal of the last especially a salutary and mortifying employment. How easy it is to be good upon paper! I felt myself humbled, even to a sense of hypocrisy, to observe (for I had forgotten the book) how very far short I had fallen of the habits, and principles, and interior sanctity, which I had found it so easy to recommend to others. I hardly read a page which did not carry some reproach to my own heart. I frequently think of a line which Prior puts into the mouth of Solomon,

'They brought my Proverbs to confute my life.'"

"Celebs in search of a Wife" had now been before the

public about ten years, and its rapid sale both in England and the United States testified its great popularity. The author's profits for the first year amounted to ten thousand dollars: a reward, as it were, for the exercise of her talents, under severe and protracted bodily suffering. "Never was more pain bound up in two volumes," she said. The work contains a beautiful portrait of woman as she should be, and we only wish there were more Lucillas for the inquiring Celebses of our own day: were there more like Celebs, there possibly might be more Lucillas, if, as in trade, the demand creates a supply: certain it is, that men in search of wives often strangely overlook those traits of character and principles of action most necessary to the happiness of married life, while beauty, wealth, or accomplishment possess a market value greatly beyond their real worth. It is curious to see how many inconsiderate marriages take place every year within one's own observation: how puzzled many a man and woman would be in answering the single inquiry, "What do you want in a wife?" "What kind of a husband will you have?" The hastiness and inconsideration with which so many enter into this most important and serious relation is one great cause of the indifference and disappointment which, oftener than we are generally aware, clouds and sours the married life of multitudes.

We would advise young men to read Celebs: they would learn from it some capital hints, excellent advice, and reliable principles, to guide them in that perplexing and anxious search, which may lead to the greatest earthly happiness, or the bitterest earthly sorrow.

Dr. Henderson, the charming tourist of Iceland, found Celebs enlivening the long evenings of many a circle in that ice-bound region; Swedish youths learned from it lessons of wisdom; it was translated into French and German: and may it not be hoped that young men and maidens, and the newly married, became wiser and better for having read it.

Nor was Russia impenetrable to her influence. The "Shepherd of Salisbury Plain," with "Charles the Footman," and several of their excellent companions, made an extensive circuit throughout that empire; and she received the assurance from a pious Russian Princess, that they were opening the way for other works of a kindred character.

India also reaped the benefit of her labors. Portions of "Moses in the Bulrushes" were presented to Miss More, written in Cingalese on the Palmyra leaf, and many of her writings were translated both in Tamul and Cingalese. Sir Alexander Johnstone, Chief Justice of Ceylon, on his return to England, visited Barley Wood, to assure her of the interest which they excited among the natives, and to bespeak a poem from her gifted pen, to be sung on the anniversary of the abolition of domestic slavery on that island. Servitude existed among the Dutch settlers of Ceylon, when it fell into the hands of the English, who at the time, guaranteed to all the inhabitants their rights of private property ; nor were they willing to relinquish this among the rest, until Sir Alexander having secured to them some important privileges from the English government, in gratitude to him, they resolved, that all children born of their slaves after the 12th of August, 1816, should become free. Miss More wrote a little dramatic poem, called the " Feast of Freedom," which was translated into the native language, by two young priests, then receiving an English education under the care of Dr. Adam Clarke. The " Feast of Freedom" became a great favorite in Ceylon, the following extract of which gives utterance, through the mouth of Sabat, holding in his hand the Word of God, to the sound and healthy sentiments which fill the whole piece :

"This is the boon which England sends,
    It breaks the chain of sin :

Oh, blest exchange for fragrant groves!
   Oh, barter most divine!

It yields a trade of noblest gain,
   While other trades may miss;
A few short years of care and pain,
   For endless, perfect bliss.

This shows us freedom how to use,
   To love our daily labor;
Forbids our time in sloth to lose,
   Or riot with our neighbor.

Then let our masters gladly find
   A free man works the faster:
Who serves his God with heart and mind,
   Will better serve his master."

"What a pleasure must it afford you, my dear Madam," wrote the chief justice to the author, "to have the power of producing such moral improvement by your writings, not only throughout Europe, but throughout Asia also! For I am convinced that your writings have had a greater effect, and have been more generally read, than any other works which have been written for the last hundred years."

The next pilgrims to Barley Wood, Miss More says, "are two very interesting and sensible Persians, who have been studying the literature, arts, and sciences of this country, and are returning home with great acquisitions of knowledge. I never saw any Asiatics before who had energy, spirit, and curiosity : these are all alive. In my garden is an urn to the memory of Locke, who was born in our village ; when they saw it, they exclaimed in rapture, ' What ! Locke the metaphysician !' They go to our different places of worship, attend Bible, and other public meetings, and seem to have fewer prejudices against Christianity than you would suppose. They particularly admire Job and Isaiah, and those parts of the Old Testament which have the most orientalism. Their figures and costume are striking, their manners very genteel. I was amused to see the Mohammedans drink a little wine. The most literary of the two wished to have something of mine as a memento. I gave him Practical Piety, which he said he would translate when he got home."

The formation and growth of the religious institutions which have so distinctly marked the beginning of the present century was a source of unspeakable gratitude to Hannah More ;—And "I sometimes regret, foolishly enough," she said, " that some of my earliest and dearest friends did not live to promote and rejoice in the wonderful prosperity of such as each particularly delighted in. Dean Tucker, Dr. Kennicott, and Bishop Horne would have been among the most zealous supporters of the conversion of the Jews, as Dr. Johnson would of the Slave abolition and the Bible and Missionary societies. Bishop Porteus would have rejoiced in the prosperity of all. To descend to so poor a thing as myself and my writings, the gratification I feel in that measure of success which it has pleased God to grant unworthy me, when so many abler and better persons have been neglected, is much diminished by the loss of the above-named, and many others, who would have taken a warmer interest in what concerned me than I deserved, and that from partial kindness. But all this is necessary, salutary, and right."

In the spring of 1818, both sisters were so much shattered by sickness, that friends suspended their accustomed visits to Barley Wood, and left the invalids to that undisturbed repose, which they greatly needed. Its benefits upon the eldest were soon apparent; both mind and body were improved, and she, under that abiding sense of "doing with her might," immediately began and prepared a small work, containing twelve short papers or essays called, "Moral Sketches of Prevailing Opinions and Manners, Foreign and Domestic," to which were added her "Reflections on Prayer," so deservedly known and admired in this country.

The first edition sold on the first day, and realized fifteen thousand dollars.

In spite of the great popularity and excellent tendency of her writings, Miss More seems ever to have made a low estimate of her merits, declaring on one occasion "that the only remarkable thing which belonged to her as an author was, that she had written eleven books after the age of sixty."

The attachment of the two surviving sisters was most tender and true; they had lived much together; their Sunday labors had been equally shared; they loved the same things, and in company had visited often and again the same places; the "sweet sense of kindred" had been strengthened by the hallowed associations of a long and endeared partnership in every good word and work, and now they two were all that were left to love of the happy band that once sported over the green at the Dominie's door, in old Stapleton. How honored a household! Blest were they among women.

As months and years passed by, each were admonished, that frail was her hold on life; and each sought to live in

23

a state of constant preparation for the last summons. Miss
Patty wrote in her account-book, " This is the last I shall
ever want ;" and every scrap of paper in her desk, bore record
of a willing and waiting spirit : yet " she is eyes, and hands,
and feet," to Hannah, who might well exclaim, " How *can*
I give thee up !"

The Wilberforces made a short sojourn to Barley Wood
in the early part of September, 1819, sure of a warm
and friendly welcome from Miss Hannah, even on a sick
bed, and from Miss Patty, animated and full of spirits as
could be, it being a difficult thing to imagine her long
either crushed or cowed by bodily infirmity. On the last
day of their visit, Patty accompanied them to dear old
Cheddar, Brockly Combe, and among the green winding
ways of the region, and then remained up long after
her usual time, talking over Hannah's first introduction to
London, with all her wonted animation. It was late when
she came to her sister's bedside, to say good-night, " Our
Wilberforce and I have had such a nice hour's chat," said
she, cheerfully. A few hours later and she awoke in the
pangs of death. " Oh, I love my sufferings," she exclaimed ; " they come from God, and I love everything
which comes from him."

Whenever the mind wandered, the ruling passion, strong

in death, issued its orders like these, " Be sure let that old woman have her shoes," " Do not forget the old man's clothes,"—intent still upon those objects which had formed her chief interest and daily business of many years.

"I have lost," said the stricken survivor, " my chief earthly comfort, companion, counsellor, and fellow-laborer. I need not tell you that my grief is exquisite. God doubtless saw that I leaned too much on this weak prop, and therefore in mercy withdrew it, that I might depend more exclusively on himself. When I consider how infinitely greater *her gain* is than *my loss*, I am ashamed of my weakness. I can truly say, however, that it has not been mixed with one murmuring thought—I kiss the rod and adore the hand, that employs it. I do not so much brood over my loss as over the many mercies which accompany it. I bless God that she was spared to me so long; that her last trial, though sharp, was short; that she is spared feeling *for me*, what I now feel *for her*, and though I must finish my journey alone, yet it is a very short portion of my pilgrimage which remains to be accomplished."

" In our numerous charity schools, she had exerted herself for thirty-two years with the most unwearied perseverance," wrote Miss More, " and I may be allowed to add (now she is gone) with great success in training up num-

bers of useful members of the community and many souls
for heaven.   Never was any private individual more lamented.   Our poor gardener said 'she had made as many
garments for the poor as Dorcas, and had as many tears
shed over her death-bed.'   Several funeral sermons were
preached for her in the neighborhood, and our neighbors
have put on mourning."

Almost every day used to come messages or applications to Barley Wood, from the poor, or sick or needy of
the surrounding parishes, in quest of relief and sympathy,
found always within its friendly gates.   For several weeks
after Miss Patty's death, no one of them knocked at the
door, or came near the house.   At last, the schoolmaster
of Shipham with his donkey and panniers came to receive
his stated supply of books for the schools.   " It is very
long since we have seen any of you," said Miss Hannah.
"Why, madam, they be so cut up, they have not the heart
to come," answered the old man mournfully.

Letters of sympathy, affection, and condolence came in
upon the mourner from all quarters, and friends flocked
around, to relieve by their kind offices that void which
none again could fill: nor does she turn aside from these
lesser alleviations, which may come upon the parched soul
like the soft and refreshing fall of the summer dew.

"Many people under a similar affliction are apt to say, that it is of too deep a nature to admit of consolation from the sympathy of friends. I am not of their opinion," said this honored disciple. "I feel the sympathy of kind and christian friends very soothing to my mind, and I bless God for affording me in his mercy and goodness, such a source of comfort."

The withered branch will not long survive,—so thought and feared the friends who waited and watched around her. During the spring and summer of 1820, she seemed gradually wasting beneath the repeated and violent seizures of her old complaint—speaking of her burning fever, "Nothing but the last icy hand will cool me," said she. "Poor Patty, I shall soon join her. I hope I shall feel the same patience and submission as dear Patty did. I have great comfort and quietness in my mind."

"I have never known," she said to a clerical friend, "much of those triumphs, which I hear of, but I have never been destitute of consolation, trust, and reliance—not that unauthorized calmness, which some deem to be always a symptom of peace to the soul."

"You have been a blessing to the world," spake one near her.

"No, mine has been but a poor little way—I *have* done

23*

nothing, I *could* do nothing. The righteousness, mercies, and merits of Christ are all in all."

"How long, oh Lord, how long," she exclaimed, in the extremity of her suffering.

"If you need all this, madam," said one of her attendants, "we may be well filled with dismay."

"The blood of Christ is sufficient : there is no acceptance for the best without it, and with it, the worst need not fear obtaining pardon and salvation upon repentance, but it must be profound *heart-repentance*."

Months of suffering passed over her, testing the sincerity and the unspeakable value of her christian faith ; her resignation in sorrow, her patience in sickness, her forgiveness of injuries, afforded a most eloquent commentary upon the blessed doctrines which it was ever the aim of her writings to enforce. But God was graciously pleased to raise up this aged servant, and again restore to her a comfortable measure of health.

In the worst of her illness, Cadell wrote to entreat her to prepare a preface for a new edition of "Moral Sketches," with a short tribute to our lamented king. "My friend wrote him word it was utterly impossible," she related afterwards, "that I might as well attempt to fly as to write. A week after, supposing me to be better, he again renewed

his entreaty. I was not better, but worse. I fancied, however, that what was difficult might not be impossible. So
having got everybody out of the way, I furnished myself
with pen, ink, and paper, which I concealed in my bed,
and next morning in a high fever, with my pulse above a
hundred, without having formed one thought, bolstered
up, I began to scribble. I got on about seven pages, my
hand being almost as incompetent as my head. I hid my
scrawl, and said not a word, while my doctor and my
friend wondered at my increased debility. After a strong
opiate, I next morning returned to my task of seven pages
more, and delivered my almost illegible papers to my
friend to transcribe and send away. I got well scolded,
but I loved the king, and was carried through by a sort
of affectionate impulse; so it stands as a preface to the
seventh edition. You will be as much surprised as myself
that this slight word should have made its way so rapidly
in these distracted times, which, the bookseller tells me,
has been the most unfavorable to literature that they have
ever known. The preface is such a meagre performance
as you would expect from the writer, and the strange
circumstances of the writing."

Neither sickness nor sorrow seemed to subdue the wonderful elasticity of her mind, ever alert to the call of duty, pressing into the service a weak and suffering frame.

Having been called upon to make some arrangements which anticipated the future, she added, " Not that I have the remotest idea of living through the winter, but we must *plan* for time, and *prepare* for eternity."

" I often think," she said one day, " that we are not thankful enough for negative mercies. I have often felt grateful that I have never been confined in a mad-house, a prison, or a court."

Thus her lips dropped manna. While slowly regaining strength, unab'a to endure either much company or great fatigue, she relieved the monotony of her confinement by composing " Bible Rhymes," pleasant little verses for the young, for whose welfare she was always tenderly concerned.

" People are too apt at an adv nced age," she remarked, " to imagine, because they were able to do but little, they were exempted from doing anything ; but our work is never finished while we are on earth, and when we have but one talent left, we must strive to the last to make the most of it."

Narrow as her sphere of active usefulness had necessarily become, she is not content to live upon her past greatness, but with diligent hand still busies herself in humbler works, which interest, but not o'ertask.

"I can find sufficient employment, which, if not splendid, is not quite useless," she writes to an old friend. "At Bristol, Clifton, and Bath, they have an annual bazaar for the different charitable societies, which, by means of contributions of ladies' different work, produces a good deal of money. You will say, that in my old age, I am brought so low as to write half-penny papers. Every year I write some such trifle. The ladies who conduct the bazaars in the different places, get these paltry papers printed sometimes on colored papers, and by selling them for a shilling, £20 have been collected in a year. I spend all my leisure in knitting garters and muffatees, a little decorated ; these, by the lady-customers giving five times more than they are worth, bring in the year no contemptible sum."

No one, perhaps, ever set more value on her time than did Hannah More, or how else could she have accomplished so much, with the various hindrances which sickness and society threw in her way ?

"What a large portion of time may be improvidently squandered !" she remarks ; "what days and nights may be suffered to waste themselves, if not criminally, yet *in-*

considerately,—if not loaded with evil, yet *destitute of good,*—how much consumed in worthless employments, frivolous amusements, listless indolence, idle reading, and vain imaginations,—and one can *never* make a right use of time, who turns it over to chance, or who lives without any definite scheme for its employment, or any fixed object for its end."

Let the young Christian ponder this : your time may be your greatest talent;

> " What wilt thou say in heaven,
>   When the Master asks, what hast thou done
>   With the talent I have given ?"

Upon this subject she again speaks.   Let us take heed.

" Through the unwearied kindness of more Christian friends than any other unworthy creature was ever blessed, I see through ' my loop-hole of retreat,' or rather hear of whatever interesting is going on. My conclusion is, that wickedness is wickeder than it used to be, and that goodness is better. Religion certainly has increased much among the higher classes in England, and perhaps still more in Ireland. Yet I will still venture to say, even to the religious world, ' I have a few things against thee.'

" With no small number of happy exceptions, I cannot

help observing the common fault of good people,—the *misappropriation of time.* I will only instance two particulars of the evil, of which they do not seem to me to be sufficiently aware,—*music and light reading.* Twenty years ago, when I wrote 'Strictures on Female Education,' Bishop Cleaves, of St. Asaph, was at Bath. He was much attached to me, though we differed on many points. Talking on this subject, he was so much of my opinion, that he wrote the following statement, which I inserted in a note in the first volume :—' Suppose your pupil to begin music at six years of age, and to continue the average of four hours a day at her instrument (a very low calculation), Sundays excepted, till she is eighteen, the statement stands thus—three hundred days multiplied by four, the number of hours amounts to twelve hundred ; this multiplied by twelve, which is the number of years, amounts to fourteen thousand four hundred hours !' I come now to the *reading.* I pass over Byron and his compeers in sin and infamy, though I have known some good people who now and then take a slice even of this highly seasoned corruption. I pass over the more loose and amatory novels, and take my stand on what is said to be safe ground—the novels of that unparalleled genius, Walter Scott. Now, I would not have it supposed, that I have not read with delight and admiration, all his poetry. This is a repast that might be taken with safety, though certainly not with profit, for it would be difficult to find another specimen of such admirable works with so few maxims for the improvement of life and manners. Let that pass; they gratify the taste, without vitiating the imagination; add to this, they were written at reasonably distant periods from each other, so that we were refreshed without being crammed. We come now to his novels, in which his fecundity is as marvellous as his invention. I have read one volume and a half, in which the powers of his vigorous and versatile mind were conspicuous; but from what I have since read in reviews, I rather see the absence of much evil than the presence of much good. I, of all people, ought not to find fault with authors for writing too much; yet I must return to my first position, the misapplication of time. Had he written before the flood, when perhaps there were not so many books in the world as he has introduced into it, all would have been well; he would have been a benefactor to the antediluvian Hilpahs and Zylpahs. A life of eight hundred years might be allowed the perusal of the whole of his volumes; a proportionate quantity in each century would have been delightful; but for our poor scanty three-score years and ten, it is too much. Nay, I under-estimate the chronology; I believe they have all been produced nearly in odd *ten* years. Now, I readily grant, that to the mass of readers the reading of these works should not be prohibited. To the gay, the worldly, and the dissipated, it is perhaps as safe, and even more safe, than any of their other pleasurable resources, being often their only intellectual one. The strong sense, lively exhibition of character, and animated style, certainly afford aliment to the mind. My remarks are limited to a certain class of readers, who have made a strict profession of religion. If, indeed, our time is to be accounted for as scrupulously as the other talents committed to us, *how will their reckoning stand ?* In the case of some, it is almost the only talent they have. Such ought to be especially careful that this one be rightly employed, as we have an awful lesson on the danger of unprofitableness."

Are not here important suggestions for those who have the training of youth ? Is there not too much time literally wasted at the piano, which might and ought to be spent in making acquisitions that will furnish ideas to the head, or useful employment to the hands ? To how many children is a music lesson a hated task. Why should fashion usurp the place of sense in this matter ? Why should not our girls be taught those things, which they will most need

24

to know if they grow up to become wives and mothers, and heads of families? Let christian parents consider well this most important subject.

On October 22, 1822, Miss More writes to a friend, " I was much affected yesterday with a report of the death of my ancient and valued friend Mrs. Garrick. She was in her hundredth year! I spent above twenty winters under her roof, and gratefully remember, not only their personal kindness, but my first introduction through them into a society remarkable for rank, literature, and talent."

Behold her now working for us, our own American Board.

" A drawing of my little habitation having found its way to New York, they have made a very good engraving of it, which their Board of Foreign Missions is selling; and they are sanguine enough to expect the sale will enable them to build a school in the distant island of Ceylon, for poor girls, which they intend doing me the honor of calling Barley Wood." A smile of gratification steals over her countenance.

"I find a good deal of time to work with my *hands*, while Miss Frowd reads for the entertainment of my *head*," she adds a while after; "and the learned labors of my

knitting-needle are now amassing to be sent to America
for the Barley Wood school at Ceylon—so you see I am
still good for something."

The history of this school is thus: the plan of a girl's
school in Ceylon was suggested to a lady in Massachusetts
by a letter from the Rev. Mr. Woodward, missionary of
the American Board, at Ceylon, addressed to the Society
of Inquiry, at Princeton Theological Seminary, in which
he mentioned that associations of ladies might be formed
in America, to build school-houses for girls, which would
cost about thirty dollars, each school bearing the name of
the association which supported it.

"I had just then," says the lady, "received a print of
Barley Wood from a relation in England; finding it much
admired and many wishing to possess a copy, I united
with a friend, who like myself was gratuitously collecting
funds for the Board, in the risk of having the print en-
graved for the benefit of Foreign Missions. I wrote to
Mr. Woodward, with the approbation of Mr. Evarts, that
the avails of my part of the engraving were to be appropriated to the building of a Bungalow, and the support of
a girl's school within the limits of his missionary field,
requesting him, at the same time, to select a site as nearly

like Barley Wood as could be found, and, as early as possible, to make the pupils acquainted with the character and works of Hannah More.

"The school was accordingly established in 1823, and the house has been used also as a place of public worship on the Sabbath. I sent copies of the engraving to Mr. Woodward and also to Miss More, who was so much pleased with the plan of a school in memory of her residence, that she immediately sent for its support ten pounds; the next year ten more; the year following twenty, besides bequeathing to it at her death one hundred pounds, which, together with the avails of the engraving, formed a fund for the enlargement and permanent support of the school."

"Barley Wood in Ceylon!" humorously responded an old correspondent, the oldest then living, Sir William Pepys, to whom she communicated the plan. "How this will puzzle some future commentator of your works! who will find some obscure tradition, that for some reason or other, most probably he will say, for the laudable purpose of disseminating religion, our author took this long voyage, and in commemoration of it, gave the name of her own residence to the school, which she evidently established in this island.

Her correspondence, at this time, was extensive and burdensome. " I see a good deal of company," she tells us, " but the *post* occupies and fatigues me, more than my guests. If you saw my table on most days, you would think were I not a minister of state, I was become, at least, a clerk in a public office.

" The mass of books and pamphlets, which I have from America would surprise you. I do not naturally love republicans, but these people appear really to be making such rapid advances, that they seem to be determined to run with us the race of glory."

The excellent Bishop Chase of Ohio paid her a visit in July of 1824, at the anniversary of the Wrington Bible Society, when with a party of seventeen others he dined at Barley Wood, still hospitably open to numerous and admiring guests. The venerable hostess was unable to appear at table, but she received the company in her own apartment, after dinner, where a long and animated conversation was kept up for several hours, in which she bore a distinguished part. Her powers of conversation even at seventy-nine were almost unrivalled ; so rich, so eloquent, so judicious, so appropriate. " You could not touch her," says one, " without finding her electrical wit, genius, and godliness—her speech was always with wit, seasoned

24*

with grace, and ministered to the edifying of the hear-
ers."

Almost entirely confined to her room, the range of her
affections is as wide as ever, and her charities continue
to flow, blessing herself in blessing others.

Besides the larger appropriations demanded by her
schools, and the various missionary and charitable objects
in which she took a deep interest, her benefactions went
into humbler and more retired channels; students were
aided in their books and education, young clergymen in
purchasing their libraries, and poor widows in eking out
their scanty incomes; twenty guineas, a legacy just received from some dignitary whose name she had never
heard, were sent to Mrs. Judson for the redemption of two
little Burmah slaves, and ten pounds were once sent to
Miss Hannah Adams, at Boston, on receiving her history
of the Jews, and learning that her efforts were made in
behalf of a widowed sister and aged father."

On the reception of one hundred pounds, from the son
of Sir William Pepys, who had for many years been in
the habit of making her an almoner of his bounty, and at
whose death his son thus evinced his reverence for his
memory, her reply admits us to take, as it were, a parting
glance at Cheddar, and a pleasant farewell of the comfort

and prosperity which, like the green grass, is creeping around the Mendip Ridge.

"I most thankfully accept the liberal sum you so generously offer. It is indeed most gratuitous on your part, and very acceptable on mine, as my schools consist of six hundred children, and the friends that used to help me out a little are dead. I do not know if I ever mentioned to my admirable correspondent that, attached to my schools, in three different parishes, I instituted thirty-five years ago a female club, for the parents of my children. I continue to give them an annual festivity, when every girl bred in my schools, and belonging to their respective clubs, if they have maintained a virtuous character, receives what they are pleased to call the bride's portion of the club-day. This envied portion does not amount to a guinea; but I think it has helped to promote sobriety. I have the satisfaction to know, that by petty accumulations and long perseverance, though the members of the club only subscribe sixpence a month, I shall leave these poor people possessed of nearly two thousand pounds in the three parishes. I have long since placed it in the funds, where it is accumulating. I have put it in the trustees' hands. The club is now no further expense to me, except the annual feast, where my valuable companion represents me.

Since my inability to be with them, to give it more credit, ten neighboring clergymen, with some other gentry, attend, and make tea for the poor women. I should not have dwelt so long on this subject, but as an instance of what *perseverance* and *petty* saving *may accomplish*. It explains how misers, with small means, grow rich by petty savings."

There is something touching and beautiful in old age with a mind unblighted by the frosts of time, and a heart warm with love to God. Childhood is lovely and confiding, but its movements are the playfulness of the kitten, and the friskiness of the lamb. Youth is strong, earnest, full of hope: it believeth all things, it willeth all things. Middle life is doubting, doing, cumbered with care, and anxious about many things. But old age—a good old age—is confiding, without being careless; earnest, without being wilful: cheerful and diligent, less anxious for to-day,—more trusting for to-morrow.

Life has gone through the spring of hope, the summer work, the autumn harvest, and now, though winter chills are creeping around the heart, and benumbing the limbs, within is glowing the heavenly flame, without the friendly warmth of human kindness. How sweetly it leans on the unseen arm; "*When* and *whether* belong to Him who governs both worlds. I have nothing to do but to trust.

I bless God, I enjoy great tranquillity of mind, and am willing to depart, and be with Christ, when it is His will,— but I leave it in His hands, who does all things well." Such is the language of Hannah More, with eighty years' experience of the goodness and grace of Him in whom she believed.

How different is this from the language of one not long departed from the literary world, of exquisite taste and loving heart, yet who knew not that peace which those have, whose souls are stayed on God. "A new state of being staggers me. Sun and sky, breeze and solitary walks, summer-holidays and the greenness of fields, and the juices of meat and fishes, and society and the cheerful glass, and candle-light and fireside conversations, and jests, and irony,— do not these things go out with life? Can a ghost laugh and shake his gaunt sides, when you are pleasant with him?"

Well may the believer exclaim, "Thanks be to God, who giveth us the *victory* through our Lord Jesus Christ."

CHAPTER XVI.

Passing Away.

EVENING shadows were fast creeping around the length-
ened days of Hannah More. Her life, prolonged for beyond three-score years and ten, was slowly and sweetly
ebbing, amid the fragrant lawns and shady groves of Barley Wood, when a strange and unexpected disclosure in
her family history, drove her from its bosom, and compelled her to find another mooring for her already frail and
shattered bark.

The extreme delicacy of her health had almost entirely
confined her to her chamber for the last seven years, and
thus necessarily had withdrawn her from a minute inspection of her household; nor could Miss Frowd, her daily
friend and companion since Patty's death, be supposed to
exercise any very thorough inspection, or strong influence
over family servants, old in the service, and long used to
the ways and wants of their mistress: but Miss More's
kindness and confidence were alike disregarded and be-

trayed. Although trained to the practice of every christian
duty, illustrated by the brightest examples of piety, breathing an atmosphere of purity and love, and pensioners upon
her bounty, her servants proved false to her trust, and
basely betrayed the interests of their too indulgent mis
tress : to fill their pockets, frauds, impositions, and thefts
were for years carried on in her kitchen ; her charities had
been diverted from their appropriate channels, orders sent
to traders which were never issued ; while their midnight
revelries began to be the scandal of the neighborhood.
Miss More heeded not, for a time, the hints occasionally
dropped in her presence, concerning the reports of her
household, until at length they became unmistakably confirmed by the confession of one of their number, when she
felt that decided measures must be immediately resorted
to. Two lines of conduct were marked out by her counsellors : one, an entire change in the domestic cabinet, and
the other, a removal from Barley Wood, to a situation less
cumbered with care. After a short, but severe struggle,
she chose the latter. The Rev. Dr. Whally offered her
his convenient and elegant house in Windsor Terrace, Clifton, where she had been long known, and was greatly
loved ; thither she concluded to remove.

"I have been quite overwhelmed by this heavy blow," she

writes to Miss Roberts. " I strive and pray fervently for divine support and direction ; but such is the variety of difficulties which await me the next month, that I sink under the thought. I bless God that I slept last night, but, like the disciples, it was from sorrow ; my kind partner in these sufferings, Miss Frowd, is, I am grieved to say, in bed with a severe cold ; this adds much to my distress. You must indeed, my dear friends, you must come and advise me. I would consult you what gentleman I shall get to stay with me in the dreaded moment of separation.

" The shocking conduct of the people below, it seems, has been long the subject of discourse with the whole neighborhood,—I alone was left in ignorance through false kindness. I am more obliged to dear Mr. H—— than I can say ; he is a true christian friend. I really think this shock has hurt my hearing and my memory."

The morning of final leave-taking at length arrived, a day of heavy clouds and bleak winds, in the changeful month of April. The servants, who, surmising a change, had now gone so far as to treat her with personal disrespect, were paid a quarter's wages in advance, by their generous and forgiving mistress, and forever dismissed from her service.

Several gentlemen, with affectionate assiduity, came to

support her through her last farewell to Barley Wood: beloved Barley Wood! whose roses and jessamines, green hedges, and sylvan bowers had for twenty-seven years breathed their fragrance, and flung their beauty upon her daily paths ;—Barley Wood, whose walls and walks were instinct with the treasured memories of the past ;—Barley Wood, where the sisters nestled together in the mellow light of their declining days, and where, one by one, like the ripened and yellow grain, they had been gathered to the eternal harvest.

Descending the stairs with a placid countenance, leaning upon the arms of beloved friends, she was led into the room below, hung with the portraits of the long gone and dearly cherished ; she gazed upon them for a few moments in deep and tearful silence ; brief and sad were the parting glances on familiar haunts, as she hurried with tottering steps towards the carriage. "Ah," she sadly said, "I am driven like Eve from Paradise, but not by angels."

Her elastic and thankful spirit was not slow to discern the beauties of her new home, which commanded a bold and delightful prospect of Leigh Woods and Nightingale Valley, with the blue Avon winding between. Her face glowed with delight, as her dim eye lingered on the rich expanse.

25

"I was always," she exclaimed, "delighted with fine scenery, but my sight of late years has been too dim to discern the distant beauties of the vale of Wrington. It has pleased Providence to ordain me, in my last days, a view no less beautiful, all the features of which my eye can embrace."

Miss More's ready and gentle acquiescence to this providential ordering of her affairs gratified her friends, and reflected peace and homelikeness throughout her new abode. "Clifton is very pleasant," she gratefully declares; "fewer cares and more comforts." A few months after the settlement she pleasantly writes to Wilberforce: "I am diminishing my worldly cares. I have sold Barley Wood, and have just parted with the copyright to Cadell of those few of my writings which I had not sold him before. I have exchanged the eight "pampered minions" for four sober servants. I have greatly lessened my house expenses, which enables me to maintain my schools, and enlarge my charities. My schools alone, with clothing and rent, cost me two hundred and fifty pounds a year. Dear good Miss Frowd looks after them, though we are removed much farther from them. The Squire of Cheddar attends them for almost the whole of Sunday, and keeps and sends me an accura,e statement of merits and wants; so that I have many comforts.

As I have sold my carriage and horses, I want no coachman; as I have no garden, I want no gardener. I have two pious clergymen, whom I call my chaplains, and who frequently devote an evening to expound and pray with my family, uniformly on Saturdays. My most kind and skilful physician, Dr. Carrick, who used to have twelve miles to come to me, has now not much above two hundred yards. As to your kind visit, we can give you two beds, and one for a female servant; I am sorry I can do no more. The house, though good, furnishes few conveniences. We have no servants hall, of course, no second table; but we are surrounded with hotels, and lodging-houses, &c. It is delightful that we shall meet once more this side of Jordan; Miss Frowd desires her best respects. She is my great earthly treasure. She joins to sincere piety great activity and useful knowledge. She has the entire management of my family, and manages well. She reads well and reads much to me. I have much more to say, and much, I trust, to hear, when we meet."

And thus are we admitted to the inner arrangements of Windsor Terrace, No. 4, to behold the domestic tranquillity of this diminished household.

But if Clifton released its venerable occupant from home cares, it opened the door to hosts of visitors, whose flittings would never have extended to Wrington. Her conversational powers, which charmed the elegant and polished circle of the last century, still retained their brilliancy and freshness; her liveliness of manner, chastened by time and sorrow, was blended with a heart-warming christian love, inspiring both old and young with confidence and affection, while many were attracted towards her by the world-wide reputation of her writings and labors. Nearly four hundred visited her in the first three weeks, which so exhausted her strength and consumed her time, that two days in a week were set apart for general visitors, her "levee days" as they were called; while to her most intimate friends she was at all times accessible.

One day in playful mood she sketched her Court at Windsor Terrace. "The Duke of Gloucester, Sir Thomas Acland, Sir Edmund Hartapp, and Mr. Harford, are my sportsmen. Mr. Battersby, Mr. Pigott, and Mrs. Addington, my fruiterers. Mrs. Walker Gray, my confectioner. Mr. Edward Brice, my fishmonger. Dr. Carrick, my state physician and zealous friend. Mrs. La Touche, my silk mercer and clothier. Bishop of Salisbury, my oculist. Misses Roberts, my counsellors, *not* solicitors, for they give

more than they take. Misses David, my old friends
and new neighbors. Messrs. Hensman and Elwin, my
spiritual directors. Mr. Wilberforce, my guide, philosopher
and friend. Miss Frowd, my domestic chaplain, secretary
and house apothecary, knitter, and lamp-lighter, missionary
to my numerous and learned seminaries, and without con
troversy, the queen of clubs (in allusion to the village
clubs already mentioned). Mr. Huber, my incomparable
translator, who, by his superiority, puts the original out of
countenance. Mr. Cadell, accoucheur to the muses, who
has introduced many a sad sickly brat to see the light, but
whispers that they must not depend on a long life."

Barley Wood was sold to William Harford, Esq., and
all her business interests were so adjusted, that no cares
were left to harass the infirmities of that period of life,
when the grasshopper becomes a burden.

Five weary years did she linger on the borders of the
river of life, and yet not weary, for her heart retained its
spring-like cheerfulness and her faith its joyful confidence,
even after the brightness of her intellect was obscured by
the damps and mists of decaying nature. Repeated attacks
of inflammatory disease in the region of the chest often
brought her extremely low, from which, through the unremitted care and faithful attentions of Miss Frowd, she

25*

again and again revived, until the November of 1832,
when the seizure became more violent, sadly prostrating
both the mind and body, and rendering the remaining ten
months of her earthly pilgrimage months of extreme
weakness, of watchful nights and restless days, unalleviated
by any hope of favorable change, except that which must
bear the spirit to its Heavenly Rest. Her pious ejaculations were the utterance of a soul, ripening for glory.

"Grow in grace," she earnestly whispered to her attendants, "grow in grace and in the knowledge of our Lord
Jesus Christ," "Jesus is all in all," "God of grace," "God
of light, God of light, whom have I in heaven but Thee?"
"What can I do? what can I *not* do with Christ? I
know that my Redeemer liveth," "Happy, happy are
these, who are expecting to meet in a better world. The
thought of that world lifts the mind above itself. Oh, the
love of Christ, the love of Christ!"

Long waiting on the shores of Jordan, "My dear, do
people *ever* die?" she said to her friend. "Oh glorious
grave! It pleases God to affect me for my good, to make
me humble and thankful—Lord, I believe, I *do* believe with
all the powers of my weak, sinful heart. Lord Jesus!
support me in that trying hour, when I most need it! It is
a glorious thing to die!"

When some one spoke of the good deeds, which had adorned her life, she quickly replied, " Talk not so vainly— I utterly cast them from me, and fall low at the foot of the cross."

Thus she waited, wearily in the body, but joyfully ; the spirit, until the 6th of September, 1833. The usual family devotions were attended at her bedside in the morning ; her wasted hands were devotedly raised in prayer while her countenance glowed with unwonted light ; she lay all day, quiet and speaking not, while ever and anon a radiance as from the land of glory illumined her sunken features. In the early night, she extended her arms calling " Patty," as if, in vision, this last and dearest of the household band had come to bid her welcome to the redeemed on high. A few more hours and she sweetly fell asleep in Jesus, on the dawning of the 7th, in the 89th year of her age. Five days afterwards, Miss More's remains were conveyed to Wrington, and consigned to the family vault by the Rev. Thomas Biddulph, Rector of St. James at Bristol.

All the shops were closed, and the church-bells tolled their solemn requiem, as a long and mournful procession followed her to the grave, joined at its arrival at Barley Wood by large numbers of the neighboring gentry, clergy, and peasantry, with multitudes of little children, for whose good, the departed had long and lovingly labored in the prime of her health and fame.

In the village church-yard, beneath a yew and willow, the traveller beholds a plain stone, marking the final resting-place of the five good sisters, and bearing the simple inscription :—

"Beneath are deposited the mortal remains of five sisters :

Mary More died 18th of April, 1813,—aged 75 years.

Elizabeth More died 16th of June, 1816,—aged 76 years.

Sarah More died 17th of May, 1817,—aged 74 years.

Martha More died 16th of September, 1819,—aged 60 years.

Hannah More died 7th of September, 1833,—aged 89 years.

All these died in faith,
Accepted in the Beloved.
Hebrews xi. 13.   Ephesians i. 6."

A handsome fortune had been accumulated by the industry and talent of these ladies, Miss Hannah More having realized from her pen alone, one hundred and fifty thousand dollars. A large portion of it was bequeathed to public institutions, whose fortunes and influences she had long followed with deep and hearty interest: among the various items mentioned in her will, we find some relating to our own land. Diocese of Ohio, £200. Books for Ohio, £50. Newfoundland schools, £100. Also Barley Wood school, Ceylon, £100. Distressed Vaudois, £180. After an enumeration of seventy-one objects, to which fifty thousand dollars were appropriated, the remainder of her property was to be invested in three per cent. consols, to increase the endowment of the new church of St. Philip and Jacob, which began to be erected in one of the destitute parishes of Bristol, numbering a population of sixteen thousand souls, hitherto without the public services of the Gospel. It was now suggested adding a school to the church, which should bear her name, and thus commemorate her memory through an instrumentality which she had used with such eminent success,—*teaching the poor.* At a meeting, holden in Clifton, on the October following, these resolutions were presented and adopted :—

" That the distinguished talents and qualifications of the late Miss Hannah More, consecrated most usefully and efficiently, throughout the course of a long life, to the noblest ends of christian benevolence, have justly embalmed her memory in the public esteem and veneration.

" That this meeting is of opinion, it is desirable to convey to posterity some public memorial of the sentiments embodied in the preceding resolution.

"That a subscription be entered into for placing a tablet to the memory of Miss Hannah More, in the parish church of Wrington, where her own remains and those of her four sisters are interred; and should the sum collected exceed what may be deemed necessary for the proper execution of such purpose, that the surplus be devoted to the establishment of a school (to bear her name), in connection with the new church in the parish of St. Philip and Jacob, in Bristol, towards the endowment of which she has bequeathed the residue of her estate."

Six thousand dollars remained after the erection of the tablet, costing six hundred dollars, which may be seen in the parish church at Wrington, bearing this humble testimony to her worth and genius :—

Sacred

to the memory of

Hannah More.

She was born in the parish of Stapleton, near Bristol,

A.D. 1745, and died at Clifton, September 7th, A. D. 1833.

Endowed with great intellectual powers,

And early distinguished by the success

Of her literary labors,

She entered the world under circumstances

Tending to fix her affections on its vanities;

But, instructed in the school of Christ

To form a just estimate of the real end of human existence,

She chose the better part,

And consecrated her time and talents

To the glory of God, and the good of her fellow-creatures,

In a life of practical piety and diffusive beneficence.

Her numerous writings in support of religion and order,

At a crisis when both were rudely assailed,

Were equally edifying to the readers of all classes,

At once delighting the wise,

And instructing the ignorant and simple.

In the eighty-ninth year of her age,

Beloved by her friends, and venerated by the public,

She closed her career of usefulness,

In humble reliance on the mercies of God,

Through faith in the merits of her Redeemer.

Her mortal remains are deposited in a vault in this

Church-yard, which also contains those of her four sisters,

Who resided with her at Barley Wood, in this parish, her

Favorite abode, and who actively co-operated in her unwearied

Acts of Christian Benevolence.

Thus endeth the outward life of Miss Hannah More.

CONCLUSION.

WE have played with her at Stapleton, studied with her at Bristol, admired her at London; we have gone with her to the thoughtful retirement of Cowslip Green, joined the sisterhood at Barley Wood, visited her schools, heard her conversation, beheld her popularity, witnessed her daily life: and now shall we pass from the contemplation of a character like hers, no wiser, or better than before? Shall it be like a tale that is told, quickly fading? Are there no lessons for *self-application* in this brief sketch? What shall the young of our own day learn from the light of her shining example?

Much of the personal influence which Hannah More exercised in the brilliant circles of literary life, was undoubtedly owing to her unrivalled powers of conversation, full of wit, sense, and originality; to these were added a penetrating and sagacious mind, which, with its thorough knowledge of mankind, obtained by a large acquaintance with almost every class of society, enabled her to comprehend the dangers to which the English masses were exposed,

from the sophistries of French infidelity and English dema-
gogues, and instantly to seize and apply an appropriate
remedy. Her tracts and stories for the times are among her
most remarkable productions, displaying as they do the
nicest perceptions of character and opinion; they silenced the
murmurs of discontent, and the doubts of skepticism,
and were like oil upon the rising waves of revolution.

Her first works upon the irreligious habits and tendencies
of the higher classes in English society, were characterized by clear and candid statements of the most obvious
and reasonable requirements of Christianity—statements
uttered with such discretion and truthfulness, that their directness could not offend, even where it was least welcome.
They were read and pondered.

As she herself came to clearer and fuller apprehensions of
truth and duty, the nature and importance of her mission
became more distinctly revealed : then followed that series of
religious teaching, that plain and faithful application of the
principles of the gospel to the heart and life, which seemed
so powerfully to quicken the spiritual life of the church,
and elevate the standard of practical piety. Miss More
felt the moral want of her times : these were general de-
clension and coldness in the religious world ; customs and
maxims had insensibly stolen upon the church, which sul-

26

lied its purity, and diminished its influence. The writings
of Wilberforce and Hannah More, warmed and enriched by
a living faith, infused new life into dead forms, and gave to
the christian profession a quickened conscience, higher aims,
and a holier life.

The intellectual gifts which distinguished Hannah More,
rich and influential as they were, formed not her chief excellence, nor that perhaps which most commends itself to
our reverence and affection. It was her *solid* and *earnest
piety* which imparted breadth and depth, strength and
beauty to her character, and made her influence felt even
to the ends of the earth. Herein is that with which we
have to do. What were the elements of that faith which
obtained so good a report, and left so shining an example ?

There is a religion of taste, which admires the beauties
of this outward world, and is awed by the grandeur of its
Maker. It is inspired more by the book of nature than of
revelation ; more by the natural than the moral attributes
of Deity ; it dwells in the imagination, high, and inacces-
sible, apart from the interests of common and familiar objects ; it seeks solitary places, and dies amid the din and
bustle of noon-day life ; it shrinks from the sin and distress
of the actual, and sighs for the good and beautiful of the
ideal ; it yearns for the dim aisles of an old past, and would

seek the aid of painter and sculptor to help it in its devotions; it is amiable, tasteful, and full of reverence. Was it the religion of taste which moulded a character like Hannah More's?

"I am a passionate admirer of whatever is beautiful in nature, or exquisite in art," she declares. "These are the gifts of God, but no part of his essence; they proceed from God's goodness, and should kindle our gratitude to him; but I cannot conceive that the most enchanting beauties of nature, or the most splendid productions of the fine arts, have any necessary connection with religion. You will observe that I mean the religion of Christ, not that of Plato; the religion of reality, and not of the beau ideal.

"Adam sinned in a garden too beautiful for us to have any conception of it. The Israelites selected fair groves and pleasant mountains for the peculiar scenes of their idolatry. The most exquisite pictures and statues have been produced in those parts of Europe where pure religion has made the least progress. These decorate religion, but they neither produce nor advance it. They are the enjoyments and refreshments of life, and very compatible with true religion, but they make no part of it. Athens was at once the most learned and the most polished city in the world, so devoted to the fine arts, that it is said to have contained more statues than men; yet, in this eloquent city the eloquent apostle's preaching made but one proselyte in the whole areopagus.

"Nothing, it appears to me, can essentially improve the character, and benefit society, but a saving knowledge of the distinctive doctrines of Christianity. I mean a deep and abiding sense in the heart of our fallen nature; of our actual and personal sinfulness; of our lost state, but for the redemption wrought for us by Jesus Christ; and of our universal necessity, and the conviction that this change alone can be effected by the influence of the Holy Spirit. This is not a splendid, but it is a saving religion; it is humbling now, that it may be elevating hereafter. It appears to me also, that the requisition which the christian religion makes of the most highly gifted, as well as of the most meanly endowed, is, that after the loftiest and most successful exercise of the most brilliant talents, the favored possessor should lay his talents and himself at the foot of the cross, with the same deep self-abasement and self-renunciation as his more illiterate neighbor, and this from a conviction of who it is that hath made them to differ."

Again, there is a fashionable religion, priding itself upon orthodox doctrines, but lax enough in orthodox practice; it is trifling, irresponsible, and florid, mixed up with frivolity and worldliness; enjoyment is the measure of duty; it seeks only to be pleased, not instructed, and in the pursuit has contracted habits which have proved snares, and imbibed tastes which have weakened and debased its principles. How is it rebuked by the strong language of earnest piety and a living faith!

"We must avoid," says Hannah More, "as much as in us lies *all such society*, all *such amusements*, all *such tempers*, which it is the daily business of a Christian to subdue, and all those feelings, which it is his constant duty to suppress. Some things which are apparently innocent, and do not assume an alarming aspect, or bear a dangerous character; things which the generality of decorous people affirm (how truly we know not) to be safe for them; yet if we find that these things stir up in us improper propensities; if they awaken thoughts which ought not to be excited; if they abate our love for religious exercises, or infringe on our time for performing them; if they make spiritual concerns appear insipid; if they wind our heart a little more about the world; in short, if we have formerly found them injurious to our own souls, then let no example or persuasion, no belief of their alleged innocence, no plea of their perfect safety, tempt us to indulge in them. It

24*

matters little to *our* security what they are to others. Our business is with ourselves. Our responsibility is on our own heads. Others cannot know the side on which we are assailable. Let our own unbiased judgment determine our opinion, let our own experience decide for our own conduct.

"As our kind of reading has much to do with the formation of our religious character, and the fostering of corrupt or correct tastes, we cannot forbear noticing that very prevalent sort of reading, which is little less productive of evil, little less prejudicial to moral and mental improvement, than that which carries a more formidable appearance. We cannot confine our censure to those more corrupt writings which deprave the heart, debauch the imagination, and poison the principles. Of these the turpitude is so obvious, that no caution on this head, it is presumed. *can* be necessary. But if justice forbids us to confound the insipid with the mischievous, the idle with the vicious, and the frivolous with the profligate, still we can only admit of shades, deep shades we allow, of difference. These works, if comparatively harmless, yet debase the taste, slacken the intellectual nerve, let down the understanding, set the fancy loose, and send it gadding among low and mean objects. They not only run away with the time which should be given to better things, but gradually destroy all taste for better things. They sink the mind to their own standard, and give it a sluggish reluctance, we had almost said, a moral incapacity for everything above their level. The mind, by long habit of stooping, loses its erectness, and yields to its degradation. It becomes so low and narrow by the littleness of the things which engage it, that it requires a painful effort to lift itself high enough, or to open itself wide enough to embrace great and noble objects. The appetite is vitiated. Excess, instead of producing a surfeit, by weakening the digestion, only induces a loathing for stronger nourishment. The faculties which might have been expanding in works of science, or soaring in the contemplation of genius, become satisfied with the impertinences of the most ordinary fiction, lose their relish for the severity of truth, the elegance of taste, and the soberness of religion. Lulled in the torpor of repose, the intellect dozes, and enjoys in its walking dream,

All the wild trash of sleep, without the rest.

" In avoiding books which excite the passions, it would seem strange to include even some devotional works. Yet such as merely kindle warm feelings, are not always the safest. Let us rather prefer those, which, while they tend to raise a devotional spirit, awaken the affections without disordering them; which, while they elevate the desires, purify them; which show us our own nature, and lay open its corruptions. Such as show us the malignity of sin, the deceitfulness of our hearts, the feebleness of our best resolutions; such as teach us to pull off the mask from the fairest appearances, and discover every hiding-place, where some lurking evil would conceal itself; such as show us not what we appear to others, but what we really are; such as co-operating with our interior feelings and showing us our natural state, point out our absolute need of a Redeemer, lead us to seek to him for pardon from a conviction that there is no other refuge, no other salvation. Let us be conversant with such writings as teach us, that while we long to obtain the remission of our transgressions, we must not desire the remission of our duties."

"A life devoted to trifles," she again says, "not only takes away the inclination but the capacity for higher pursuits. The truths of Christianity have scarcely more influence on a frivolous than on a profligate character. If the mind be so absorbed, not merely with what is vicious, but with what is useless, as to be thoroughly disinclined to the activities of a life of piety, it matters little what the cause is which so disinclines it. If these habits cannot be accused of great moral evil, yet it argues a low state of mind ; that a being who has an eternity at stake can abandon itself to trivial pursuits. If the great concern of life cannot be secured without habitual watchfulness, how is it to be secured by habitual carelessness. It will afford little comfort to the trifler, when at the last reckoning he gives in his long negative catalogue, that the more ostensible offender was worse employed. The trifler will not be weighed in the scale with the profligate, but in the balance of the sanctuary."

Are there not many, who may well take heed? Remember how much is implied in your Christian profession ; what interests, both for time and for eternity, are at stake. Will you be content with the "beggarly elements" of a worldly religion, when God demands a holy life?

Still farther : earnest piety prevents that *skepticism*, which is liable to creep into the soul at a certain stage in the religious experience, and which if not expelled chills and corrodes the faith, until one has only a name to live. Have you not known many, who entered upon the religious life with the fairest promise? How lovely was the first blossoming of piety! what prayers were offered for their continuance in well-doing! what hopes were entertained of their usefulness! Time elapses, and alas! how is the fine gold become dim. They have lost their confidence ; they

see no use in that wherein they once delighted ; their love
is cold, the.r faith is low, their hands are feeble : they are
weary, discouraged, faint-hearted.

Why this folding of the hands, this feebleness of the
faith ? Amid the first exercises of the renewed soul, the
work of a christian life is beheld through the bright
medium of joy and hope : there is no account laid with
remaining corruptions within, and discouragements and
trial from without ; believing all things, hoping all things,
the warfare is begun. What various hindrances beset the
way ! what disappointments chill his heart ! what sins
still clog the soul ! He may have learned to labor, but not
to *wait :* while planting the seed he looked for the harvest.
This forms the great crisis in the religious life, when in the
waning light of our first love to God, we first fully *realize*
all which that love demands : when the *ardor of feeling* is
to be replaced by the *steadfastness* of principle : when the
life that has been given us, no longer dependant upon the
nurture of christian friends, must henceforth depend upon
ourselves—*our* watchfulness, *our* labors, *our* care, must
alone nourish it, strengthen it, and bring it to the stature
of a perfect man in Christ Jesus. From this day of labor
and of trial, alas ! how many shrink ;—who is sufficient for
these things ? cries the fainting believer.

"I can do all things, through Christ strengthening me"—responds a living faith, which bears the soul through its doubts and fears, and teaches that hardest, last learned lesson, yet dearest and best of all, that in yielding *a willing obedience to God, and striving to do his will,* He *will work in us* both to will and to do of his own good pleasure—Christ in man.

This is the substance of an earnest piety : of a working, saving, living faith, beautifully and impressively illustrated in the life and labors of Hannah More.

Who is striving after it ? who will go and do likewise ?

THE END.

Printed in the United Kingdom
by Lightning Source UK Ltd.
123464UK00001B/46/A